*These stories remind us that each and every student can succeed, regardless of zip code, skin color, native language, gender/gender identity, immigration status, religion, or social standing. We thank these brave students for touching so many in our community by opening up and sharing their most private struggles.*

—Dr. Kristine McDuffy, Superintendent, Edmonds School District

*Writing is a path to mutual understanding. The honesty and strength that comes through in these stories gives me hope that we can continue to learn from each other. The Scriber Lake writers embody what Ray Bradbury said: "Let the world burn through you. Throw the prism light, white hot, on paper."*

—Maria Montalvo, columnist, *Edmonds Beacon*

*Book seven is the best volume yet of this highly recommended series for your personal library. Ten authors pen personal examples of the value of learning from past experiences, planning our future and targeting our goals. These writers demonstrate that focused, courageous action overcomes fear.*

—Bob Fuller, Rotary Club of Lynnwood

*I can think of no better way to teach students than to have them craft and publish their own stories. After including student voices and the Scriber books in my classroom for six years, I know that storytelling unites and heals us. This writing program should be part of every school's curriculum.*

—Stacy Wright, teacher-librarian, Edmonds School District

*These students have woven their resilience into the fabric of the entire school community. We must read these stories so that we can foster a collective consciousness.*

—Karen L. Mikolasy, professor, University of Washington

# LISTEN

# LISTEN

young writers reflect on

**chaos
clarity
action
balance**

Compiled and Edited by Marjie Bowker and Leighanne Law

STEEP STAIRS
PRESS

Compiled and edited by Marjie Bowker and Leighanne Law

Copyright © 2019 by Scriber Lake High School

For information, contact:

Steep Stairs Press
23200 100th Ave. W.
Edmonds, WA 98020
425-431-7270

www.steepstairspress.com

www.facebook.com/steepstairspress

ISBN-13: 978-0-9974724-2-4

Library of Congress Control Number: 2018912753

Cover design by José Pulido
www.pulido.co

Nahui Ollin Aztec transformation cycle image in Introduction courtesy José Gonzalez and Xicanx Institute for Teaching and Organizing (XITO).

Editing by Tim Holsopple

Print book and eBook formatting by Hydra House Books
www.hydrahousebooks.com

We dedicate this collection of stories to Liza Behrendt, who helped all of us align our deepest truths with positive actions.

Liza Behrendt

1965–2018

Scriber teacher, 2010–2018

*See Ariel Sanabria's story, "Freebird," written in honor of Liza (page 98).

*Listening is a magnetic and strange thing, a creative force. The friends who listen to us are the ones we move toward. When we are listened to, it creates us, makes us unfold and expand.*

—Dr. Karl Menninger

Books published by Steep Stairs Press:

*We Are Absolutely Not Okay: Fourteen Stories by Teenagers Who Are Picking Up the Pieces* | 2012

*You've Got It All Wrong* | 2013

*Behind Closed Doors: Stories from the Inside Out* | 2014

*We Hope You Rise Up* | 2015

*I'm Finally Awake: Young Authors Untangling Old Nightmares* | 2016

*This Is a Movement: Owning Our Stories, Writing Our Endings* | 2017

*Listen: Young Writers Reflect on Chaos, Clarity, Action, Balance* | 2018

# WRITING TOWARD CLARITY, ACTION, AND BALANCE

**Scriber writers from 2012 to 2018 reflect on the writing process:**

*Writing helped me battle my demons and move forward after years of hiding behind shame and fear.*

*It should've been hard to put myself back in the mindset of my trauma, but writing it out felt more cleansing than anything else.*

*The cycle of abuse and trauma has been addressed—which is revolutionary, not just healing.*

*I felt empowered to share my story. I felt as if I brought light to the shameful past and learned to accept it.*

*The thought that someone could relate to my story and not feel alone with their own story motivated me.*

*Writing helped me process what happened. Reading it afterward put me back in that vulnerable state and I could go through it with clearer eyes.*

*Writing my story helped me forgive myself for things that I've done.*

*My story forms an instant connection between me and the person who reads it.*

*Having a specific time in the day where I could focus on writing my story—instead of having it race through my mind all day—helped me focus more on school.*

*Writing my story helped me become more engaged with the community.*

*Scriber helped me figure out who I am and who I wanted to be just by loving me.*

*I no longer have the nightmares, and the thought of what happened doesn't put me in a weird mood and give me the sickening feeling I used to get.*

*I am more stable and controlled. I can handle my emotions better and keep myself from slipping into depression again.*

*Writing my story prevented me from committing suicide.*

*At first it didn't feel real, but now I realize I stand behind something with the potential to change perspectives. Now if I feel emotionally wrecked I just write.*

# TABLE OF CONTENTS

# INTRODUCTION

At Scriber Lake High School, we believe that listening is one of the loudest forms of kindness, and that healing begins the moment a person feels seen and heard.

For seven years, Scriber students have been writing about deep emotional pain, and for seven years, Scriber staff have been trying to improve how we listen to them. We have processed and shared unimaginable traumas as a community, raised our consciousness, and increased our collective empathy. Over a seven-year period, our school has become a place where all stories are welcome, and many students have chosen to make their stories available to the world with the hope of providing healing to others.

This year, the Nahui Ollin Aztec transformation cycle (see image on following page) provided a deeper intentionality and metacognition to our writing process. Each writer was introduced to the graphic and was asked the guiding questions; our job was to listen as they analyzed their experiences, then reflect back what we heard. Through this process, they learned to listen to themselves and discovered a wealth of self-knowledge about their own placement within the cycle. For example, Emily Yalowitz ("The Bench") writes from a place of gaining clarity, Brian Macedo ("Respeto y Responsabilidad") writes from a place of taking action, and Moniline Winston ("Rising") writes from a place of balance.

Compassionate self-analysis provided emotional distance from their trauma, allowing them to make important distinctions about who they are, what they've been through, and who they want to be. The stories you are about to read reflect each student's travelogue around this transformation cycle—holistic written portrayals of journeys from darkness into light.

Each year, our current writers build on the courage of those who wrote

1

**Stability**

**Analysis**

Gained knowledge that serves to make us stable and balanced human beings. We must constantly draw on that precious knowledge to bring about beauty in our everyday lives.

Place of darkness, chaos, creation. Represents our subconscious mind where we can sort things out a place and time of reflection and introspection.

Quetzalcoatl

Tezcatlipoca

Huitzilopochtli

Xipe Totec

Our actions must reflect that positive transformation. With new perspective we must act positively and move forward in a positive manner.

Place of cohesion and order to our thoughts whereby clarity is reached as a result of reflection. Through our reflection perspective is gained and our thoughts transformed.

**Positive Action**

**Transformation**

*Nahui Ollin Aztec transformation cycle.*

## Questions for each writer:

### Analysis (Chaos)
Where have you been?
Where are you now?

### Transformation (Clarity)
Where do you want to be?

### Positive Action
How will you get there?

### Stability (Balance)
How will you know you have arrived?

-2-

before them, which explains the increased level of honesty and vulnerability of the stories in this book. Decisions to include details about sexual abuse and suicidal ideation prompted difficult yet soulful conversations between writers, parents, teachers, administrators, and counselors. We discussed whether the inclusion of these painful details would bring more positives into the world than negatives.

In the end, the writers themselves decided that only the deepest honesty would bring transformational healing. The details remain because we chose, once again, to listen to them.

We know that today's behaviors are guided by our visions of the future. In her best seller, *Grit*, Angela Duckworth cites passion and perseverance as two qualities necessary for making these visions a reality. By embracing and participating in the transformation cycle, these authors have taken steps to free themselves from trauma and have demonstrated the passion and perseverance to create the lives they envision.

Each story is full of light, heart, and soul.

We are so grateful we were invited to listen.

Marjie Bowker and Leighanne Law

# THE BENCH

## EMILY YALOWITZ

"Let's get out of here," my English teacher says.

We walk out of the classroom, through the back doors of the western wing, through the metal gate, and away into the trees. Sunlight shines through gaps in the branches and we listen to the birds singing their freedom. We reach the park and head past a gazebo. Kids play in the field and it smells like summer is on its way.

Escaping through the woods with my English teacher is a little strange, but Scriber Lake High School is cool like that.

I came to Scriber because I thought I wouldn't be successful at any other school. I've never been successful. I can never focus. I have ADD, and teachers are always stressed over me not doing work. Everything was great at the beginning of the year because I met more people and was more social than I had ever been before. But nothing changed academically; I still couldn't focus, and teachers still didn't know what to do with me. I was failing math spring quarter and it was too late to try to make it up, so I decided to work on my story for the Scriber book. My English teacher suggested it. She said I had an interesting writing style, which made me feel like I was good at something.

When we first started working on it, she showed me the Aztec transformation cycle and explained the four steps: analysis of the chaos, clarity, positive action, balance. She asked me where I was in that cycle.

"I have no balance," I told her. I explained that whenever I get to feeling content for a while, something screws it up, whether it's me or not. That there is no balance in my life, no middle ground, only highs and lows. My life feels like a ball of yarn; I travel through each strand, gaining the hope of escape, but the tip of it is tied in a knot.

I told her I'm not comfortable, not even in my own home. "I want trustworthy, supportive people in my life," I said. "I want to have a better home. I want to take my education seriously. I want to be drug free. I want to be positive. I want to be pure."

She looked at me for a while, then suggested the walk.

When we get to a bench, she says, "Let's sit here. We'll call this 'Freedom Bench.' We're going to talk about how you're going to set yourself free on this bench. But first, tell me about the chaos."

So I start at the beginning. I go into detail about what happened when my mom went from opioid painkillers to heroin when I was nine years old, to the present, where I am depressed and sad and looking for escape every single day, longing to be free. I tell her in fragments, from memories too vague for much detail. Just the ones that stand out.

I'm nine years old and it's evening. I'm starved for my mom's attention. I walk down our creaky wooden hallway towards her door, dragging along the feeling of dread deep in my stomach. The door is usually locked, but this time the handle turns and when I open the door I see my mom sitting on the bed with a needle in her hand. The room is warm, gloomy, and full of negative energy. One lamp on, the small TV on low volume, and the curtains closed.

She rushes under her green covers.

"Get out!" she yells, sounding both aggravated and guilty.

It's my tenth birthday. It's a sunny day at Wilcox Park and everyone is trying to keep me occupied.

Only three out of fifteen of my friends show up, but I'm cool with it. All that matters to me is food, presents, and fun. But someone more important than my friends isn't here: my mom. Eventually she shows up with my grandma and plants herself in a chair away from everyone. She has nothing to say, not even to me. She's completely loaded.

Everything smells of pizza and fresh cut grass and a hint of nerve. After two hours go by, I eat food and open presents, then find myself alone with nothing to do. I try to join my uncle and my friend's game of tennis and realize they don't care that I'm here. I take a hint and head up the hill to the woods. I sit down on the dusty ground for a while not thinking about anything for once. About thirty minutes go by and no one even notices I'm gone. I go back down and find that my mom is gone. I feel a rock in my throat, like I can't swallow.

I'm relieved when I finally get to go.

A few weeks after my birthday party, my parents and I are sitting in my mom's red Chevy truck in the QFC parking lot on 196th. It smells of cigarettes and heroin. They sit on soft Tinker Bell seat covers in the front seat and argue as I sit in the back and listen. I don't remember much from the argument, but I do remember my mom threatening to leave us. I begin to cry because I want to drown out their yelling, but they keep on raising their voices like cats getting ready to fight. They are so loud their voices begin to scratch up.

A few weeks later, my mom is in treatment. My dad and I come to visit for the first time, and we are led to her dorm-style room. There she is, sitting on a twin sized bed, brushing her hair. Next to the bed is a nightstand with her toiletries and a small lamp.

She's been here two weeks and I can tell she is on edge, going through withdrawals. Her skin looks clear, though.

I remember crying because I didn't want to leave her.

A few years later I learn that she remembers me screaming and having to be taken away, and that the memory kills her.

The next time we visit she is smiling. It is the first genuine smile I have seen on her in months. She shows us her AA Big Book with people's writing all over it, and it's apparent that there is some sort of inside joke to call each other "sexy bitch." Her roommate is sitting on the other bed rolling a cigarette as she politely eavesdrops on our conversation.

We decide to take a walk around campus. It is a sunny day and all of the patients are involved in activities. To the right of us a group of people are playing volleyball in a sand-filled area, and to the left people are soaking up the sun in a small field. My mom leads us to a peaceful forest area where a small creek runs through the middle and benches line the side. We sit down and relax. My mom is smiling. She is with the people she loves. She is happy. She is pure.

Shortly after my mom returns from treatment, I am in the kitchen making ramen and I hear my mom's muffled voice talking to her sister on the phone in her room. She walks out of her bedroom door and makes a beeline to the garage. She's about to open the garage door when she tells her sister that she has been drinking vodka.

"Mom!" I shout.

She jumps back. She didn't realize I was in the kitchen. Her eyes widen with a "busted" look.

"Don't tell your dad," she says as she opens the heavy door to the garage and slams it shut behind her.

My face tenses and I can feel my jaw drop.

*She's doing it again.*

*She's relapsing over and over again.*

First heroin and now alcohol. I know the history of this. After my mom graduated from high school, she began to drink and do lots of drugs. Eventually, she stopped after she became friends with my dad. And my dad stopped, too. She and my dad got married and had me. But nine years later, she's doing it all again.

I am at a loss for what to do.

Two years later, my parents have split up, and my mom and I have our own apartment. My mom has been drinking in front of me since we moved in, and it's only getting worse.

One evening after school I am in the living room watching Netflix and I hear crying coming from my mom's bedroom. I am afraid to find out what happened, but I slowly walk down the hallway toward the sound of her wailing. My stomach sinks when I see her sitting on the floor beside her bed. On the desk next to her is a bottle of wine and a bottle of vodka. I rush down to the ground to comfort her. She's talking to me but I can't tell what she is saying. She begins to laugh maniacally before passing out and hitting her head on the nightstand.

"Mom! Wake up!" I yell.

I yell and shake her until she finally wakes up again. The cycle continues for about an hour until I decide I can't sit with her all night. I drag her to the bathroom so she can relieve herself, then leave her alone for about a minute until I hear a loud crash. I run back to the bathroom and see that she has fallen off the toilet and into the bathtub. I drag her from the bathtub to her bed and lie down with her. She cries as I hold her. Eventually she falls asleep around 2 am.

I feel tired and disappointed. The next day she apologizes and tells me she won't drink vodka anymore.

It's the middle of my freshman year and my mom has been grounding me for months for sneaking out. It's getting worse and worse. I feel trapped. Being grounded and having everything taken away just makes me feel more trapped and all I can think about is getting away.

I'm at my dad's house because my mom asked for his help.

Everything feels like too much. I can't handle it. I have to get away.

I tiptoe out of my room and into my dad's room as he sleeps. I unplug his phone and slip it into my pocket. I go out to the living room and log into my Facebook account and message my friend to come pick me up, pack four days worth of clothes, write a note to my dad, and leave through the back door.

My friend is there. "I'm running away," I say. We drive down I-5 listening to Nirvana and Metallica, and he drops me off at another friend's place where I stay the night. I don't sleep at all because of how nervous I am about my dad waking up the next morning to find I'm not there. I think about how he will feel, how my mom will feel. I leave the next morning and walk to yet another friend's place.

But I can't stand it anymore. I message my dad.

*"i'm okay dad. i love you"*

*"Emily. Where are you. I will call the police and do the NCIC thing with posters and the whole 9 yards if you don't tell me where you are now. And make yourself available to be picked up immediately."*

*"please dad i need space"*

We message back and forth until I tell him I just want to sleep and he agrees to come pick me up. When I get in his truck, he doesn't speak a word to me. He takes me back to his house and lets me sleep for five hours. That night I tell him how nervous I was knowing how he must have felt and that I don't want to do that to him again.

And now I am here, one week after my escape, sitting on Freedom Bench with my English teacher.

It's not just any bench. It's a bench drenched in sunshine. It's a place where I can imagine anything and there is no stopping it. It's a positive place that has been here for quite a while, and will stay here, waiting for the future.

It's a destination where I can think about having a life without any escapes...no pot, no alcohol, no sneaking out. No thoughts of dying. A life filled with passions and music and happiness.

A place where I can put some pieces together and make a plan.

"I have an idea," I say after we've talked about my chaos for long enough.

"What is it?" she asks.

"What if I write this part of the story and leave the reader hanging to see what happens next, in the next book? Like maybe I could write in every book until I graduate."

She thinks for a while before answering. "I love that!" she says. "Then they can see your path to that place of balance. I really love that. So you'll write your story from the Freedom Bench, where you are trying to gain clarity."

She's a little more excited than I am, but I answer, "Yeah."

### A Note from Emily

Shortly after writing this, my grounding was lifted because my mom and I were able to make a compromise. I began to have hope again and was able to see my best friends for the first time in months. Writing about this has helped me see things from my past much clearer; writing it down made all the puzzle pieces fit together. I am also more focused on my mom's happiness. She just graduated from community college with a degree in small business and has been able to send in a few job applications. She is on her way to a better place, and I know she accomplished this for both of us. I wrote this to get to a place of balance and clarity. I'm not there yet, but at least I have started on that path. If you have had to deal with a family member or close friend that abuses drugs and/or alcohol, you aren't alone. Don't turn your focus over to them and let it affect you. Find your balance. Find your clarity. Find your purity.

# RESPETO Y RESPONSABILIDAD

## BRIAN MACEDO

"Be confident," my dad says when I hesitate at the edge of the river. "The horse will know it if you're feeling nervous or scared and will not do what you want."

I poke my horse until he starts to go. I can feel his muscles flex as he walks on the rocks, the cold water splashing on my boots and jeans.

Halfway across, my dad turns to wait for me. "Come on," he says in his deep voice.

The sky is bright blue, the birds are circling around the bird feeders, and the grass is lush and green on the other side. I take in the moment because I can't believe I am actually here, heading to my grandfather's cabin with my dad for some target practice.

For the past two years all I've had is a picture of him in my wallet from my fifteenth birthday, almost two years ago. He, my mom and I had just gotten out of Mass and my dad was wearing things he wouldn't usually wear: a nice button-up shirt, a jacket, and snakeskin boots. My mom looked like a queen in her long, beige dress with silver sparkly trim, and I was standing in the middle in a shirt and tie, completely unaware that in a few months my dad would be gone.

Whenever I look at the picture all I see is something I will never get back.

But I'm with him now, for five days, in Jalisco. El Chilacayote is the small town where my mom and dad met before they came to the US, where I was born.

He's been back here since he was deported.

I had always heard stories about this place, but now I'm seeing it for myself—the town where everyone knows each other and where bells ring three times every Sunday for church. It takes one and a half hours to get to a city for groceries and haircuts from here, and four hours to get to Puerto Vallarta for a pizza.

I'm trying to enjoy the moment, but how can I enjoy the moment when deep inside I know that I'm going to have to leave in a few days? How can I feel good if I have been feeling horrible at home without him? How can I enjoy every second with him if all I feel is emptiness? *"I've been through things that I won't never probably heal from"* —the lyrics from "Dying Inside" by JayteKz go through my mind. I don't think I will ever heal from the day that ICE surrounded us and took him away.

My dad waited for me outside wearing his black and red checkered pajamas, a big, grey sweater and worn old slippers. The air was cold and I could see the cloudy reddish sunrise behind him.

"What are you doing?" I asked.

"I'm warming up the truck for my Prince," he said.

I rolled my eyes. *Oh my god. Why do you have to call me your Prince?*

On our way to school we had to stop for gas, so we turned left at an intersection. In my dad's rearview mirror, I saw four black cars—a Jeep, a Ford F150, and two Tahoes—race through the red light behind us.

*What's going on? Why aren't they getting stopped?* I thought.

I turned to get a better look at them when I realized that all four cars were circling around us. My dad swore. We stopped.

When the officer approached the window I knew he wasn't a regular cop because he wore all black: a black vest, black boots, a rifle strapped around his shoulder and a black logo that read "ICE."

I froze. In a panic, I looked at my dad, who was staring at the officer.

The cop shined a flashlight in the window at us and around the inside of the car, then tapped on the window with it.

My dad hit the button to roll down the window.

"Are you Juan Macedo?" the officer asked. My dad looked from me to the officer, then back to me again. I usually spoke English for him.

"Yes," I answered quickly. "Why, is there a problem?"

"Sir, please step out of the vehicle. You have a deportation order."

My dad turned to look at me, and I realized that days before, when my dad told us he saw ICE officers waiting outside the house, we should have believed him. My mom and I told him that it was probably the cable guy. But here they were, surrounding us. I knew by the look on his face that I wouldn't be seeing him for a long time.

I felt tingly, light, and filled with butterflies. *Is this really happening?*

As two officers opened my dad's door, he got out and gave me a serious look, like he was letting me down. He took his phone out of his pocket and put it on the car seat, then handed me money from his wallet. "Here's some money if you need it," he said in a low, sad voice. "Take care of your mom."

Another officer came to my side and opened my door and said, "Will you please step out of the vehicle?"

My hands got sweaty as I grabbed my dad's phone and wallet, then stepped out.

Two officers handcuffed my dad and led him to one of the blacked-out Tahoes.

As the four cars drove away, I paid closest attention to the Tahoe that had my dad in it. In seconds I couldn't see the car anymore; it just blended with the darkness of the morning. Everything started to sink in.

I turned and started to walk home as the sun rose, tears running down my face. Deep inside I felt like I was dying. My only thought was *How am I going to tell my mom?*

My dad is wearing the same black "FOX" hat he's always worn. When he takes it off to wipe the sweat from his head I can see that his salt and pepper hair is starting to recede. He's like a big stuffed animal; he looks big and mean, but he wouldn't hurt a bug. He's super nice to everyone and is really goofy. He always sends me cute text messages with cartoon dogs and other characters.

We come to a fence and my dad dismounts. He opens the gate, turns and says, "Don't be in-between the horses. If your horse gets too close to my horse, he will kick."

*No he won't*, I think to myself. But I obey and step aside. About four seconds later, my dad's horse kicks mine, just like he said it would. He pulls his horse through the gate.

"I told you," he says.

I've learned that it's usually worthwhile to listen to my dad. When he left, I took over his landscaping business. He told me that if I could make it work, I could have it. For the past two years, I have gone to work every day at 7:00 am, no matter what. I pay bills, look after my mom, and don't do the things my friends are doing, like go to parties and stay up late. He also told me that people would try to take advantage of me because of my young age, and to stand my ground when it happened. I was nervous when he said that, but I thought that if I was upfront about the price, there wouldn't be a problem. Of course, he was right. It happened just like he said it would, just a few months into taking over the business.

When I pulled into the long driveway surrounded by tall green bushes, it was 7:30 am. As I parked next to a blacked-out Escalade, a yacht, and a three-car garage, I thought, *This is going to be one of the hardest days of work.* It was a big cleanup and would involve twelve hours of trimming, weeding, and laying out mulch. A $750 job. My partner couldn't make it, so I was on my own.

I got to work right away and finished the front by lunchtime, took a short break to go to the dump and for teriyaki, then came back to start on the back. The owner and three of her friends came out and started tanning on the deck, drinking and hanging out by the river. They were laughing and playing while I busted my ass.

*If I work hard, I'll have days like that someday, too.*

Around five I went to the dump again and brought back two yards of mulch for the front. After I was done laying it out it was around 7:25—I had worked for twelve hours. I was covered in dirt and sweat. I knocked on the door and waited for the owner to come out. She didn't answer, so I turned and started walking toward my truck.

I heard the door open and the woman ran up behind me. "How much will it be?" she asked.

*Oh no,* I thought. I had told her the price over the phone, but it was harder face to face.

"$750, like we agreed," I answered in a low, nervous voice. I noticed that I stuttered, too, and thought about what my dad had told me about customers being a pain in the ass to deal with.

The vibe tensed. "Could you take $600?" she asked. There was a change in her voice—kind of a squeak at the end.

My hands started to sweat. "No, we agreed on $750," I said. My ears felt warm. I was mad at myself. My dad had told me to stand my ground firmly if something like this happened.

"Well, it didn't take you as long, and it was only you. The agreement was for two of you," she said. She was getting into my head. Her stringy, blonde hair hung in her face, and it bothered me that her makeup didn't match her skin tone.

"I've been working all day by myself because he didn't show up. But got everything done," I answered, trying to sound confident.

"Hold on, I'm going to call my husband."

I leaned against my truck and dialed my mom to tell her the situation while the woman spoke in quiet tones with her husband, one hand on her hip, the other on her phone. She took small, nervous steps side to side in her Louis Vuitton sandals. She also wore Ray Ban sunglasses and a gold watch.

Then she turned to me and spoke more loudly so that I could hear her. In a very condescending tone, she told her husband, "He's too scared to make a deal. He has to call his mommy."

Adrenaline rushed through me. I tried to make eye contact with her but she wouldn't look at me. I started laughing. I couldn't believe what she had just said.

She passed the phone to me.

"We'll give you $600 and you can keep working for us," her husband said, "or we can pay you the $750 and you will lose us as clients." Because of his deep voice, I imagined him to be over six feet tall and built.

But what she said about my mom made me mad enough to stand my ground. "I want the $750. We can lose you if that's what you want. We don't work for stingy customers."

I heard the dial tone from him hanging up, and handed her the phone.

"So what did you decide?" she asked.

"$750."

"We will mail you a check," she said. She turned, walked to the house, and slammed the door behind her.

"Thank you," I called after her. *Whatever.*

I got in my truck to go.

When I drove away, I felt anger mixed with pride. I had been trapped in a cell, but I didn't fold under pressure. I had stood my ground. And I knew I would do it the next time, and the next. I kind of wanted it to happen again. *My dad would be so proud of me.*

❧

"Be ready because we are going through a place that is blocked by a log," my dad tells me. "Make sure to duck your head and move your rifle to the side so it won't pull you away."

As we get closer to the log I try unsuccessfully to stop the horse. I panic. I duck and move my rifle as fast as I can, but the old rotting log knocks my hat off as I ride under it.

My dad stops, dismounts and picks up my hat because he knows I struggle to get back on the horse. He hands it to me and says, "There's a clear path up ahead." We move on and I take in the beauty; everything is so quiet and peaceful. We go around a curve and find ourselves in a clear opening—we can see the town, which is a long way from where we started. We are surrounded by bright blue sky with no sign of clouds.

I've never seen anything like it.

My dad used to always talk about his vision of him and me running the landscaping company together. "I will be the old grandpa with a bald head driving the big trucks around and you can collect the checks," he would say. "Just give me my $500 and I'll be set."

As we stare at the view, I feel lost knowing I'm going to have to leave soon, and that his vision can never become reality. My dad won't be there to guide me, or to see my success. I'm scared for what will happen to him, and I'm nervous about my family's future, my future.

"You didn't do too bad for your first time. You'll get used to it," my dad says, breaking into my thoughts. For a moment I think he's telling me I'll get used to life without him. Then I realize what he's talking about.

"Yeah," I answer. "I will."

### A Note from Brian

I have been growing my landscaping business for two years now. Keeping my dad's company going has been rough, but I have learned many new things, like how to talk to strangers, and how to stand up for myself with experience to back me up. At first I didn't want to write this story because I felt uncomfortable sharing what happened, but after I started writing, I felt a lot of relief and it became easier to explain to others. When people relate to my story, I feel both sad and happy; I feel sad because I know how much they have suffered, but I feel good knowing my story has made them feel less alone. My goal is to graduate this year and go to Edmonds Community College for Landscape Design.

# PLANKTON

*noun* : an organism that everyone has adapted to feed on

## MINDY FILLA

My hands are shaking as I rub them on my grey sweater, an attempt to rid them of the sweat that has accumulated since the bell for third period rang. The halls are a raging river of faces and backpacks—constant and angry—everyone flowing around each other, like fish, for nearly four whole minutes. Pools of people gather around the bottoms of the stairways, unbothered by the closeness to others. I am plankton, small and microscopic, drifting and floating as the waters carry me from one side of Edmonds-Woodway High School to the other. I can feel my heartbeat in my ears, drowning out the threatening hum.

*Is it noticeable that I'm shaking? Am I walking weird because of it? Do I look as terrified as I feel?*

The familiar taste of blood fills my mouth as I chew on my already raw lips. I have the urge to bite my fingernails, but bringing my hand up to my mouth would attract attention to me. As I'm biting the inside of my cheek, I wonder how my face looks, all scrunched up. The thought sends a wave of panic through my already trembling body, and I look around for an exit, everything becoming way too much to handle. The water's rising, and if I don't get out soon, I'll drown. I have to avoid eye contact at all costs. It's too personal, too close. The last thing I need in this moment is eye contact with any of the students who are unknowingly causing my heart to beat so fast I'm afraid it's going to burst and my lungs to contract, begging for air.

*I need to be alone. I need to get away. Too many people are looking, seeing me.*

*They're probably not even giving me a second thought, probably couldn't care less. Am I a narcissist? Why can't I stop caring?*

*I wonder if they can tell that my mind is having a war with itself.*

In the wild, making eye contact with the wrong animal can be deadly, and I've learned that the school environment and the animal kingdom are similar in that way. Keeping my head down and avoiding eye contact is what I'm best at; I need to if I'm going to survive.

This was especially true in third grade when I found myself being bullied at school. No matter where I went, there was torment. No matter how long I spent inspecting the floors or the thread of my shoelaces, someone somewhere was ready to strike. And I know that what happened all those years ago is the basis for why I am stuck in this cesspool of anxiety now.

I stepped onto the bus and exchanged a quiet "hello" with the bus driver, then quickly walked to my assigned seat in the back as he clicked away at his counter each time a student boarded. Sliding in, I squished myself against the side, wrapped my hands around my backpack, and rested my head forward against the seat. The backpack of the person sitting next to me brushed against my arm as he turned to talk to his friend, but I didn't bother looking up. The meaningless conversations circulating around weren't enough to distract me from what was going on in my head.

*I just want to be home. I hate being on edge all day, tiptoeing my way around and trying to avoid what I can't predict. I'm hiding, and still get found and made fun of for things I can't help. There's nothing I can do to avoid being pushed around during recess and called names at the lunch table. I'm so tired of it.*

I finally propped my head up and took a look around to bring myself out of the haze. A wind dancer advertisement caught my attention out the window, and as my head turned to follow it, I heard, "Don't look at me."

The harsh voice came from a girl sitting behind me. Startled by her hostility and the unwanted attention her words brought, all I could do was stare.

"I said don't look at me, creep!" she yelled more loudly.

I quickly turned around and shrank down into my seat.

*Please don't say anything. Please don't yell. Don't make it worse.*

A few moments passed with little reaction from anyone else, so I thought I was in the clear. *Maybe this once, the situation won't escalate like all the other times. Maybe this time, it'll be over fast and the other people who love to terrorize me won't join in and attack.*

As I put my backpack over my shoulder, ready to make my escape, I felt my hair being messed with and heard laughter erupting behind me.

My thick, thigh length, dirty blonde hair lived its life as a poofy mess. It was big and had no curl definition. Just one big poof. Kids always poked fun at my hair, so when I felt the girl's hands in my frizz, I was embarrassed and ready to cry.

I shot my hand up to my head to cover whatever she did and felt a glob of wet stickiness.

*They had marshmallow bunnies at lunch for Easter*, I remembered. I realized she must have put the marshmallow in her mouth, chewed it, and put it in my hair. *Everyone's gonna see it when I walk off the bus, and they will all laugh.*

My tears welled up. I saw the blurry buildings of my apartment complex pass by slower and slower as we pulled up. I shuffled down the aisle, holding my hand over the gooey mess. A few giggles still erupted from the back of the bus as I felt their eyes burn into my hand against my head, everyone wanting to catch a glimpse of what the girl had done. My heart raced and my cheeks flushed bright red. I let the tears fall, not caring.

*I just want to get out of this twenty-foot yellow torture chamber.*

The water is up to my neck, lapping at my chin. Everything is too much. The suffocating hallways seem so much smaller when you think about how many eyes could be on you, judging you. The C wing bathrooms are up ahead. I need to get out of this whirlpool. I feel like I'm risking my life by trying to weave though the people swimming against the current to reach the bathroom, but when the water reaches my lips my body finally takes control of itself. I cut off two girls lost in conversation to enter the bathroom with my head hung low to avoid any sort of confrontation. I can't look up to see who's washing their hands when I enter, and walk swiftly to the last stall and lock myself in.

The noise of an air dryer fills the echoey space, and soon the door closes. I'm alone. It's silent, finally. My heart is still thumping wildly in my chest and all the muscles in my torso ache, but I'm alone. Checking my phone, the dim screen tells me it's only been three minutes since the bell rang. The water is receding now, breathing isn't as hard of a task, and I'm no longer in danger of drowning. My unsteady palms, slick with sweat, cause setting my phone down on the toilet paper dispenser to be a much louder act. Much louder than I can handle at the moment, in the daze of the panic. Now, the aftershocks kick in. My arms begin to itch and burn.

There was another layer to my third-grade nightmare that started me on this path to self-destruction. School was not the only place I was tormented; there was also a stranger at home who made my life hell. I couldn't escape. There was no safe space for me.

"Can I use my DS?" I asked my dad. I figured he was done with it because it was sitting on the table next to his beer can.

"No," he answered passively while continuing to stare at the TV.

"You've had it all day," I said, cautiously. "Why can't I use it?"

He was living with us for the first time after eight years of living without him. Life with him was an endless minefield. Every day I had to worry if what came out of my mouth was going to set him off. I longed for when it was just my mom, siblings, and me, and I could breathe without fear.

He stood up. "Don't talk back!" he screamed in my face, then added, "You're just an ungrateful brat, you know that? Always asking for things from me."

I ran to my room, away from his harsh words, feeling nauseous from smelling the mix of Bud Light, body odor, and chlorine from his poor hygiene; he considered our pool to be his daily shower.

Three episodes of *Say Yes to the Dress* passed as the last bit of daylight filtered through my hot pink curtains. I couldn't retain any of the details of the dresses because I was too focused on listening to every noise that came from his "spot" on our couch, hoping he wouldn't come into my room.

*I hope he'll just let me lay with mommy tonight like I used to before he moved in*, I thought, *like I did when my brothers and sister were still living with us and we had too few bedrooms. I miss that.*

The snap of the DS told me he was still angry, and the noise of it left my ears ringing. A tired creak came from our cat-scratched, brown couch and my stomach tightened with every step I heard coming down the hallway. I dropped my head when the door opened, avoiding his stormy blue eyes.

There was a beat of silence before he spoke, his voice rigid and cold. "Your mom's almost home, get ready for bed."

"Oh ... okay." My voice came out small; I was afraid to set him off again. I was hoping for an apology when he poked his greasy mop of dirty blonde curls into my room, but I wasn't quite sure why.

*He's never apologized for being mean or yelling at me these last few months. Why would I hope for anything different now?*

He closed my door without another word. I let out a sigh as I stood up and walked over to my dresser. My Bobby Jack pajamas comforted my uneasiness for bedtime. The pink and green swirls surrounding the monkey matched the flower decals on my walls.

When I got back into bed and pulled up the covers, the bells on our front door jingled, letting me know she was home. I ran out to give her a quick hug and kiss goodnight.

"Hi honey, how was your day?" she cooed.

"It was fine ..." I answered. I was never sure what to say, all I knew was that I didn't want her to be mad at me as well. I went back to my room feeling empty.

An hour went by and my eyes still wouldn't rest. All I could think about was wanting to be next to my mom. When the whole house was finally quiet, I slowly got out of my bed and onto the floor. I crawled my way to my mom's door frame, peering in to see two lumps in bed. I made my way in silently, between the footboard and dresser, to the small space on my mom's side of the bed. I laid down and waited for the right moment to reach my hand up to touch her in a way that wouldn't startle her. Just enough to let her know I was there. I started to drift off, and when my arm fell, it thudded against the bed frame.

"What the fuck are you doing in here?" my dad screamed. I went cold for a moment, then picked myself up and tried to escape fast enough to make everything okay, to show I was sorry. I wanted to make it back into my bed before he could strike me.

But he jumped up and screamed, "Come here! I'm gonna beat your ass!" and started chasing me down the hall.

I was screaming "no!" and "I'm sorry!" as I jumped onto my bed and tried to push myself as far as I could into the corner against the wall, hoping he wouldn't reach me. But he grabbed my leg and pulled me toward him, flipped me over and started spanking me over and over with no breaks, leaving no time for me to react to the last blow. I kept begging for him to let me go, but he didn't care. He was tired and livid. Finally, I wriggled out of his grasp and held pillows up to block his blows. Nothing worked; he slapped the pillows out of my hands so easily, and because I was struggling to try to get away, I couldn't stop his hands from coming down.

When he finally grew tired and had let out all his aggression, he walked back to my mom's room and slammed the door closed. I just laid on the bed and cried until the adrenaline was gone and I was left with aches and heavy eyelids.

*I can't even walk through a hallway without breaking down and needing to run away,* I think, condemning myself. I'm fighting my urge to gain physical control over my mental pain.

I'm missing class again. More work to make up. More assignments to add to the ever-growing list. Last time I looked I had 187 missing assignments—I just stared at it and cried. We aren't even close to being done with the school year. I've dug a hole that just keeps getting deeper daily.

*There's no way to get out of it, I'm stuck. I won't pass any of my classes, again.*

"You can fail two classes and still graduate," I remember them telling us at the freshman orientation. I have failed every class so far, and I don't know how I let myself get like this. In middle school, I was placed into honors based off my test scores from the previous year. For a short time I envisioned myself being on top of school, in honors, doing Running Start and possibly even graduating early, going to a university somewhere and taking sophisticated classes, no problem.

But here I am in this bathroom stall, failing again.

Here I am, unable to make eye contact, answer simple questions in class, or even do a presentation without quaking.

I never thought I'd struggle like this. I never thought I'd want to end my life like this. I planned so much for myself less than a year ago.

But here I am, I'm struggling to even see myself walk out of this bathroom.

**A Note from Mindy**

On the night of graduation, I received my diploma and walked off stage with forty-nine other amazing people who all struggled through their own issues and traumas to get to that point. We streamed out of the theater with pride and relief. As the crowds filled the hallway and swirled around me,

I realized how far I had come. I wasn't scared and was only overwhelmed by love, support, and congratulations. At Scriber I was able to find myself and gain confidence. I found a home. Now I walk through these hallways unafraid of anything. I can talk to anyone. I have transformed from plankton into a human being who is headed somewhere in life. Even a year ago, the thought of writing this story terrified me. Marjie's second period English was my first class at Scriber, and ended up being the class that changed me the most. Her free-writes were a safe haven for me to let out my feelings. That's what made the idea of writing this fathomable, and ignited a desire to work to overcome some of my fears. Writing this was a year-long process; there were months I couldn't touch it because it was too hard to be in the headspace it required. The days that I wrote, especially when I was working on my second flashback, left me recollecting all the details and pain. It was very difficult, but now I have a better understanding of what happened; I have clarity regarding how everything affected me, and that knowledge has helped me to move on. Next year I plan to go to Edmonds Community College, and from there to Evergreen State College. I want to study art, psychology, and writing, and eventually become a therapist who uses art to help clients cope with past trauma.

# A LOVE I CAN'T EXPLAIN

## DELAUN SMILEY-TATUM

"*Hello Delaun, here are a few pics of what we hope will be your 'new home town'!!!*"

I sit and stare at the words on the screen and the images of the Butte College campus in northern California.

*Is this really happening?*

"*I think you will love it here. Please let me know if you have questions. I look forward to hearing from you soon. Thanks, Coach Lopeteguy.*"

My dream is getting closer and closer. The words on the screen hand me a ticket to my future and I feel the stress, because I know I will have to work really hard. In my head, I'm there—I can visualize it—but I'm not there, yet.

I feel I'm out of time on everything. I'm nineteen and I'm a year away from graduating, credit-wise. But my love for football outweighs everything. The tattoo on my shoulder is an angel, a football, and the words, "A Love I Can't Explain." I really can't. All I know is that I've loved it my whole life, and this is my chance.

The last time I felt I had a chance at my dream of playing professional football was when I was a freshman at Meadowdale High School, and my coach was Mike Don.

❧

*It's time to wake up and go hit the weights*, I thought when my alarm went off at 5 am. It was pitch black and I was covered in blankets. I got up off of the recliner and turned on my speaker and put Lewie on, then got in the

In a matter of seconds she got in front of me and threw a couple of swings at my face, so I pushed her.

"You're going to hit me?" she said.

"I didn't hit you. I pushed you so you'd stop hitting me."

It was time for me to go. I walked out of the house with all the things I could carry in a garbage bag. I rode down the hill to stay with my closest friend, Keelan. Days and days passed. I just couldn't live with my mom. It wasn't easy. Months passed, switching and bouncing from house to house. At one point living in a children's group home was my way of saying that's home. But that soon came to an end. I couldn't take it.

One day my brother Tyrell called. "I heard about what you and your mom are going through," he said. "I think it's best you come and live in California."

I called my mom and told her what Tyrell had said. Two weeks later, I was off to live in Antelope Valley; there was no turning back.

When I saw the lights and felt the heat flowing through my body I knew I was a Cali kid. It felt good to be there—the presence itself was amazing. But sooner than soon I started school, my junior year of high school. My brother kept my head straight, and I felt like I had a good life. Good grades and attitude changes. Most everything about me had changed. At AV I could play football, go to the same high school as Tyrell, finish school, and have a male figure in my life. Being with him, I felt like I respected him in his house. I had structure. He checked up on me. Not like with my mom.

When we got in arguments, Tyrell would tell me, "Stay on track, don't end up on the streets. It's a bad thing. Focus."

After seven months, I sat down with him and told him I felt like I could move back and make the life choices that I couldn't make before. I thought I could bring what I was doing in Cali back home to my mom's house.

Unfortunately, it didn't work out the way I planned. I wasn't capable of staying with my mom, so I decided to stay with my oldest sister. I went back to Meadowdale High School for a little while, but slowly my grades went down again. Since I had moved around so much as a young boy it was easy for me to just switch schools or homes. I decided to attend Lynnwood High School for my senior campaign and finished the football season. But it was just a repeat of everything. I didn't attend and I failed more classes. As I saw myself falling there, I made the drastic choice to move schools again, but this time I knew I was going to a place that felt like home. Scriber Lake was a place that could change lives. It was a place where I could make my own structure and become my own man.

The email on the screen makes me think of my future.

I imagine myself waking up with a mindset when I'm on that campus. So much will depend on the people around me. Some of them could be in the same position I'm in, or maybe worse, schoolwise. But I will be around people with the same football goals as me, and if I feel like I have a place where I'm comfortable and can go further in life, I'm going to be motivated.

I want to be the person who changes the game, like Odell Beckham Jr., one of the greatest receivers of our time, known for one-handed catches. That's what I want to do. I want to break records. Change people's lives. When I look at football players, I think I can do what they do, speedwise, catching-wise.

I really need to get up to go to school so I can do what I want to do in life. All I'm hearing in my head is "you need to graduate."

No one in my family has graduated. What will it mean? That everything is lifted off my shoulders. My mom will cry, break down. "You made it," she'll say. My brothers will be proud.

I will be moving on to the next chapter, and I will be able to tell kids, "You better go to school" and "focus in."

### A Note from Delaun

At first I decided to write for the grade, but I ended up falling for the process of writing this story. It didn't really feel good to look back on five years of failures, but it felt good to know I was somewhere where I can finish my education and know I'm going to succeed. It forced me to break down the last five years of my life and helped me clarify my goals. Writing it opened my eyes to the fact that my living situation and lack of money or knowing the right people affected my opportunities. Even though I didn't go through the traditional football system, I'm still getting a chance, and that means everything to me. My message to teachers is to know your students, because usually there is a story. My message to students is to follow your dreams.

### Coach Don's Response

Delaun,

Reading your story was a real refresher for me as a coach. Hearing those things makes me remember why I do what I do and how much as coaches we can impact those around us whether we realize it or not.

I am so proud of you and how you are making strides towards accomplishing your goals not only in football but in life. You were always a talented young man and just needed to have a little guidance in your life. You are capable of things beyond your imagination. Remember that one day football will come to an end. It happens to all of us at some point. You have to think about what your purpose in life is going to be. My purpose in life is to help shape young students and athletes into hardworking and dedicated adults. What is yours going to be? As you continue to grow and improve as a person always remember where you came from, but never look back at it as a negative. Look at it as a part of how you became who you are. Continue to look into the future and figure out what it is going to take to accomplish your goals in life. Whether you reach the pinnacle of your goals or not, it is about the process that you took part in to get there. I myself did not reach the pinnacle of my goals as a high school athlete or college athlete. I did, however, give myself the opportunity to walk away from the game and know that I worked hard. I am a better person because of the things that I did and learned during my time as an athlete and a student.

Finally, I want you to know that even though I was unable to stay at Meadowdale and had to move across the state to be with my wife, I will always be your coach. If you need anything don't hesitate to reach out. If you need someone to talk to, someone for encouragement, someone to celebrate accomplishments with, or someone to help you stay on the right track, I am just a phone call or text away. Good luck at Butte—I am certain you will work hard and accomplish your goals.

Coach Don

# I WISH I HATED IT

## BRIEAUNNA DACRUZ

*Yeah come through,* my dealer's text reads. *I got that ice and brown. What do you need?*

*The usual, I got $50 on it,* I respond.

Excitement washes over my body as if I'm already high.

I'm driving with my co-worker, Brian, next to me on the Mukilteo Speedway. It's nighttime and both of us wear matching khaki pants and red-colored shirts with a Papa John's logo on the front. We're laughing at the fact that we almost just got hit by a hearse.

"If he would have hit us, we might have been riding in that," Brian says.

My heart is beating even more quickly as I pull off the Speedway and pass the airport, my speed matching it. I see the QFC ahead—my dealer is standing by the entrance in front of a table. I turn into the empty parking lot.

"I'll be right back. I owe my friend some money," I say as I park far enough away so Brian can't see what I'm doing. I hate lying to my friends and family to mask my addiction, but after two and a half years of recovery and relapse, I only seem to be lying more each time I choose to get high.

I decided to relapse again right after my shift ended—the 10th or 15th time I've lost my sobriety since April 30, 2015, just two days after my seventeenth birthday. I knew the drill. I knew who to text or call and definitely where to go.

I take a look around and throw my dealer a $50. Casually, he slides the bag of clear across the small black table.

"Yep. Have a good night. Hit me up when you need more—it's that fire," he says, slurring his words in his low, slow, quiet voice. I turn and walk back to my car with my mind on only one thing.

Two and a half years ago, on that first day, I would have never believed that "one time" would lead to this drug being the most important thing in my life.

❧

"Fuck, Jenay, let's get high. Not no weed high or anything we usually do." I pulled my white hoodie over my head and listened closely for a reply from my best friend, who was sitting across from me in a blue recliner identical to mine.

With a chuckle and no hesitation, she answered, "What do you mean, dude?"

I knew she'd be down for a good time.

We were sitting just ten feet from the street under her grandmother's partly covered carport watching cars drive past. She tapped her left foot faster and faster and crossed her right leg over her knee. Her oversized sweatshirt covered her auburn/blonde messy bun.

"I mean my mom has some brown," she continued.

I couldn't tell if the wind gust was creating chills down my spine and goosebumps on my arms or if it was the thought of December 7, 1999, the day my grandfather was released from jail. After a year and a half sentence he was given heroin laced with something that caused him to overdose and die just three hours into his freedom. After he died, my mom sat in a depression for nine years, blaming herself and filling that void with painkillers. Ever since, the thought of needles has made me sick to my stomach and dizzy to the point of passing out. I'd spent 365 days of each of those nine years terrified that the same kind of thing would happen to her. My mom is my best friend and number one support.

"Not funny. You know what happened to my grandpa," I said. "That is one thing I told myself I would never touch."

"Well, I know there's clear, too. What are you trying to do, Bri? What's wrong?"

What was wrong was that my heart had been completely torn open by someone I loved and I just needed something to ease the pain for a moment. I avoided her question. "Clear?" I asked. "What does that do?"

Jenay turned her chair back from the table where she was loading a bowl in her Pyrex baby blue and white pipe. "Bri," she said guiltily, "'Clear' is short for meth. It's like a supercharged Adderall."

I had started taking Adderall when I was fifteen, orally, or through my nose after I crushed it into a fine powder before snorting it. It gradually got worse; I went from doing it once or twice on the weekends to eventually every day.

"Dude, let's do it. Fuck it."

I stood and followed her through the basement door that led us to her creaky carpeted staircase and up to her bedroom. As I walked through the door and approached her bed I noticed a slight bump under the blankets. I pulled the pink sheet back to see a handheld black torch, a faintly colored pink bubble, a used needle, foils both clean and dirty covered with heroin residue, and a pack of Marlboro Black 100's. As I started to move everything aside to sit on the bed, she came from behind me to do it herself.

"My mom always has her needles around and out. I don't want you to get poked," she said. She had lived with her mom in this small, nicotine-smelling, white-walled room on the top level of her grandmother's home for seventeen years, her whole life.

I sat against the wall as Jenay grabbed a lighter from the nightstand and joined me on the bed with her legs crossed.

She held the black torch in one hand and the bubble in the left. Small, fluffy-looking clouds and an odor like cat pee flowed out of the tiny hole on the top of the bubble. She used the torch to heat the clear up, slightly under the glass.

*Hisssss.*

She leaned toward me with the bubble, then stopped.

"Bri, you have to promise me this is a one-time thing. I can't be the reason you started doing this if you don't stop. I will make sure I stop, too, because it's not a good thing. We can't do this."

"Yes, dude. One time. I don't want to be a meth head. I just want to try it," I told her.

Without further hesitation, she continued. "Suck slowly, don't hold it in! Immediately blow it out," she said in a concerned tone. I suddenly realized that she looked empty, as if the drug had already taken her a while ago. I never even knew she was doing meth at all, but it crossed my mind that the twitch in her jaw and her jittery ticks were all related. I let the thoughts fly past.

While twisting the bubble back and forth between my chapped lips, I inhaled, then followed with an exhale that instantly filled my body with butterflies.

The feeling brought me back to when I rode the Panic Plunge drop tower at Silverwood Theme Park—that same drop of unexplainable butterflies, but even better. Hit after hit, we passed the bubble back and forth as I tried to learn the technique of hitting it the right way. I realized how invincible this made me feel; the adrenaline washed over my entire body. I felt like Superman. I no longer felt pain; I was a whiteboard that had once been covered in black marker. The hits wiped everything away and made everything empty again. I felt pure love, better than ever. Better than the love I had lost.

*Isn't that what love is supposed to do?*

Escaping reality seemed to only be possible with drugs, and this one had proven itself in just a matter of seconds.

My head was slammed with one thought.

*Does smoking more make this feeling even better?*

Without one thought of anything or anyone I loved—my parents, my nieces, my family, friends, and, to say the least, myself—I had no care in the world unless it was more of this drug.

"Let's go pick up more," I said. "Where do we go? I have money." My words came out so quickly I didn't think she understood them. Jenay didn't look too high, or maybe I was just too high to notice. She looked at the emptiness inside of the bubble.

"Bri, you said just this one time ..."

"Fine, I'll go get some myself somewhere," I answered defensively, angry.

She knew I would drive to the 128th Home Depot in the parking lot in Everett and find it myself. That's where we got all of the other drugs: Adderall, coke, Xanax, heroin for her mom, alcohol.

At a loss for words, she texted the dealer I didn't know she had.

*I can't wait to get more,* was the only thought that consumed me. As we began to get ourselves together and leave, my phone vibrated. It was my mom.

*Call me please.*

But I never called. I had never lied to my mom until that moment. In that short amount of time, the drug had become more important than my mom.

I grabbed the pack of Marlboros from the bed and followed her down the stairs, which seemed to creak even more loudly than before. I lit a cigarette, grabbed the aux cord and played S. Dot's song "Drugs"—"*Now I'm off this loud/so bitch please get out your feelings*"—through the speakers of my Kia Sportage. It was the perfect song for our situation, driving on cloud nine toward more clear.

Brian stays downstairs with my mom as I climb the stairs to my bathroom, lock the door and stand on the Seahawks football rug in front of the sink. I take a small piece of toilet paper and shake the bag of clear out onto the toilet paper. My heart skips a beat. I know I'm going to feel amazing once I wrap it into a small ball and puddle water into my hands, then place it inside of my mouth to swallow.

I walk out of the bathroom door already feeling the adrenaline and casually make my way back down the stairs and into the garage where my mom and Brian are smoking. My mom thinks I've been sober for five months, but in all reality I only remained sober for one week after my fourth and final rehab.

"Hey, want to take a hit?" Brian asks, and I grab the bong. I have to act as normal as possible, so I add this drug onto the other. My body is jittery and I keep talking faster and faster, which I am very aware is one of the biggest giveaways.

I'm doing everything in my power to hide my high; I've become an expert at it. I have to be, because I have two parents who have battled addictions themselves. Otherwise they wouldn't have been blindsided for eight months before sending me to an adolescent lockdown treatment facility in Oregon three years ago. While I was there, I wrote my dad a letter telling him his drinking was bothering me, and that I didn't like the way it made him change while I was growing up.

"I'll do what I can, I promise," my dad had told me in response during one of their weekend visits. "But you have to promise me the same. If you try your hardest, I'll try my hardest." My dad had never let me down on a promise that would benefit me. The best thing about this promise was that he benefited as well. He overcame his addiction for me.

Now I'm breaking my promise to him, and I will do anything to hide it, even as my mind is shutting down into blackness. I make my legs take me away from them and up to my room.

Somehow, to this point, I have not only succeeded in hiding it from my parents, but have escaped legal trouble again and again.

I had no other choice but to pull over into an empty Home Depot parking lot and wait for the second my life would be over. Six months and twenty-seven days clean all for nothing, only to relapse and arrive at another crucial moment.

The lights seemed to be getting brighter and brighter as a tall man with a blue state patrol hat approached my car. My friend Gerardo sat in the passenger seat, swearing under his breath. My heartbeat sped up the closer he got. I realized that the lights were not getting brighter, there were just more of them. Three police cars were circled around us. I thought about all of the things in my car: meth, a torch, a bubble, an ounce of weed and a pipe. Plus, I was high. This could mean years in prison.

"Gerardo, you have to hide the bubble, we're going to jail," I said as my body began to tremble.

He shoved everything inside his pants. "I'll take the blame for everything," he said. He had already been in trouble with the law and he wanted to keep my record clean.

I rolled down my window and put on my best sober face.

"Hello. How are you doing tonight?" the officer said in a conversational tone. "Did you happen to know who was in the white vehicle that was trailing behind you before I pulled you over?"

I realized a few of my friends had called the police after following me for two hours, from Mountlake Terrace to Sedro-Woolley, because I wouldn't get in their car. They knew I had relapsed and were worried about me.

"I do," I said as calmly as I possibly could. I knew I was convincing.

"I pulled you over tonight because ..."

*You're going to jail* were the words I expected to come from his mouth.

"... because she called us and said you were drinking and driving."

I couldn't help but chuckle out loud; I couldn't believe they had lied. If they had told him I was on meth, the police would detain me and search my car. They would have found the bubble, torch and clear.

"Absolutely not. I was just having a rough night and came down here to visit a friend I haven't seen for awhile. Now I'm headed home to Seattle."

I exhaled a sigh and my whole body relaxed until he flicked his big silver flashlight into my car and eyes. My pupils were so dilated they must have looked like they were going to pop out of my head.

*My life is over*, I thought once again.

"Well, from what I can see, after following behind you before I pulled you over, your driving did not seem impaired. You do not appear impaired or smell like any trace of alcohol. So I have no probable cause to pull you out of the car. But I need to see your license, registration, and insurance."

*No sobriety test? No breathalyzer?*

With my heart still beating, I reached for all of the documents and handed them to him.

When the cop left, Gerardo and I sat in silence for a moment. I knew my record was clean, but Gerardo's record wasn't. "If he comes back, I'm running for it. I don't want to go back to jail again," he said.

"Don't do anything stupid. We've got this," I answered.

All I could think about were my nieces, Amelie and Camilla. They had begged me not to leave, but I had chosen meth over them and in place promised them I would be there when they woke up in the morning. They were only three and four years old. They were the most important people in my life since they were born and were a big reason I got sober in the first place. They were getting old enough to understand things. If I didn't come home, I would break not only that promise, but so many more for years to come.

In a few minutes, the cop returned, handed me the papers and said, "It's late. Get out of here and drive safely home. Have a good night."

"Thank you! Have a nice night," I answered as he walked away with the lights still flashing. I looked to the left of me and saw them, my friends, parked right next to Wendy's watching to see what happened. She knew I was twacked out, not drunk.

I didn't know whether to be upset at them for calling, or grateful for the lie.

A text came through as soon as the officers were out of sight. *If you don't head straight home and to rehab, we're going to notify state patrol again and tell them the truth*, it read.

*Okay*, I texted back. I had no choice.

I collected myself as Gerardo and I exchanged a look of relief. I put the car in gear and drove back onto the road that never seemed to end.

Little did my friends know as they followed me home that the next trip to rehab would do nothing to change my life. I wished I hated this drug, but I loved it. The first hit after relapsing made my love for the drug grow so much more than before, and it controlled everything I did.

I sit alone on the edge of my bed in my white-walled room nodding my heavy head over and over for hours.

I'm nodding into death, falling into the blackness with one little spot of light that I feel I'm going to reach.

*Should I tell my mom?*

*Should I face my choices alone?*

*If I get out of this, how many chances will I have left?*

My legs are weaker than they've ever been, but I make myself walk to the other side of the room and open my safe where I keep my drugs. I look inside the baggy from my dealer and see that the clear that I've already taken from is coated with blackish residue.

*Heroin?*

*Like my grandfather.*

I ball up my fists in anger as I swallow the clear, not caring, bringing myself even closer to death. There is no way I am throwing away my drug even if it is laced with heroin, the drug I swore I would never do.

*My family will remember me as a drug addict.*

I imagine my dad's voice receiving the phone call telling him I'm gone while he's miles away in Alaska, my nieces' heartbroken faces, and the possibility of them following in my—and my grandfather's—footsteps, my mom discovering my body and the words she has said to me so many times. *"If I lost you, I would have no reason to live."*

I feel the sensation of my soul leaving my body.

I'm in a tunnel. Death is an existence, not a person.

I can see it, and I'm about to touch it.

## A Note from Brieaunna

This is my third story in the Scriber books through Steep Stairs Press; however, writing this one was a much different experience than the others because I wrote it over a two-year period. I began writing it while I was in active addiction, trying to get somewhere positive by letting it out onto paper. My title, "I Wish I Hated It," was decided during that time, because from day one I wanted to hate it more than anything. The process of getting my story out and finished was my first step to sobriety; I knew it would finally give my family some answers to the questions surrounding my addiction. I am now twenty years old, over a year sober, and each 30th day of the month I add more time to that total. After three attempts, I finally graduated last June. I knew if I were to live past that last, terrifying moment of my addiction, I would have no more chances. It was live or die. My girlfriend, Katerina, was the one who kept me from my downfall, both emotionally and physically. Every day since, she has made me believe that life has a purpose. Being loved and loving back was a huge part of my healing process—maybe the hugest part. Everyone else in my life only interfered with my sobriety, so I chose to remove those toxic people by deleting all social media back in November 2017. At that point I started to grow in a great way, into the person I fought to be for so long. Surprisingly, it was the best and easiest decision I have ever made. Now I will go off into the real world with a diploma I never thought I would receive, and I have plans to start college so I can get my life back into my own hands. I am no longer detained by a monster. I finally broke free. To anyone who is struggling with addiction: know that it may take you one try or one hundred tries but there is a good light at the end of the tunnel of addiction. Everything I learned through my willpower to continue fighting and writing made me the person I am today. I am no longer holding my secret behind my back—I am letting it out for you and everyone else.

# FAILURE, FAILURE, FAILURE, FREEDOM

## JOEY WALKER

*My story is as raw as it gets. I included graphic details of my depression, cutting, and suicide attempts because I felt if I left out the details, I would still feel the weight of it and it wouldn't really be my story. If you are teetering on the verge of depression or struggling with cutting, come back to this story when you are in the right place to read it. It will be here for you.*

### FAILURE #1

"I'm going to go biking with my friends," I told my mom.

"Okay, but don't stay out past dark," she said. She was sitting at her desk on her phone, as if it were a normal day.

*I won't ever be out past dark again*, I thought. But I answered, "I know."

"Have fun!" she said, cheerfully.

I didn't answer. Instead, I grabbed the keys and walked out the door and to the garage. I pulled the door up and wheeled my bike out.

*Today is the day.*

I locked the garage, ran back to the house and put the keys inside. Then I started the six-mile ride to the bridge over 164th Street.

After what seemed like hours I could finally see the bridge, but I still had to ride down a huge hill and back up to get to it. Picking up speed I was aware of the wind and all of the cars next to me as I felt adrenaline pumping through me, building me up for what I was about to do.

When I arrived I kicked the stand out on my bike and put it next to the end of the bridge. I walked slowly onto it and looked over the railing at all of the cars passing twenty feet below to the left. Directly below me was only tall grass.

*I'm going to jump in the grass. I don't want to be seen immediately.*

My heart skipped; I had a severe fear of heights.

*Damn, it's a far drop.*

*Am I really going to do this?*

And then, clarity.

*It's far enough for this.*

I took a deep breath and climbed up onto the railing, feeling peaceful and light about the thought of not having to deal with another tomorrow.

*This is what I want.*

When I jumped, the air around me felt soothing as I dropped.

When I collided with the ground my legs slipped out from under me. I hit my tailbone and back on the ground.

Everything went black.


FAILURE #2


Coming home from school in the car, I felt more depressed than usual.

My mother said, "Are you doing alright?" I had not realized that I was showing my feelings. I was trying not to because my mom was very perceptive.

"I'm doing good enough," I said.

"You can talk to me if you need anything," she said, but I didn't want to talk to anyone.

"I know," I replied, and the rest of the car ride was silent.

When we arrived at home I quickly left the car so I could get inside as soon as possible.

*I don't think I can do another day like today,* I thought.

I didn't have friends at school other than my girlfriend, so I never talked to anyone except for the thirty minutes at lunch with her. My anxiety level was higher than usual. A feeling in the back of my throat, kind of like a constant pressure at the top of my neck, had been with me all day.

*Team Fortress 2* kept my mind busy for a few hours, and before I knew it, my father asked if I wanted to go to dinner with them.

I checked the time. It was around 6:30. "I don't want to go out tonight," I told him.

"Alright," he said. "We will bring home some leftovers for you."

After my parents left, I made the decision that I didn't want to deal with the nausea, the dread, or the constant tiredness anymore. I walked down the hall to the stairs and climbed them, then took a left into my parents' bathroom, knowing exactly what I was going to do. In the mirror I saw a sad excuse of a human being: a sleep-deprived person who hadn't showered in a few days, with greasy, messy hair.

Pill bottles were lined up next to the mirror.

*Should I do this?*

*Of course I should, it's what I've wanted for a long time. It's the only thing I've wanted.*

I grabbed a bottle of what looked like painkillers, twisted the bottle open and looked inside.

*More than enough for this.*

I dumped about fifteen of the pills into my hand, leaving just a few in the bottle, then filled a nearby cup with water.

I brought the cup up to my mouth, let out a sigh, popped a few pills, and swallowed. One of the pills got stuck at the back of my throat, so I drank some more water to get it down. I filled my mouth with water again and popped another, and another. I did this until I ran out of pills in my hand.

When I was finished, I looked in the mirror again and felt a small sense of relief.

*It's over. I actually did it.*

I felt happy that it was all going to finally end. I smiled a little and when I saw my smile in the reflection, I started to laugh. I laughed and laughed and laughed. Then I stared at myself in the mirror some more. I normally felt weak, but at that moment I felt the happiest I had been in so, so long.

I walked over to my parents' bedroom window and the sound of cars whirring and birds squawking seemed more intense than usual. I looked around the depressing, white room, then, after a few minutes passed, I walked over to my room.

My bed looked really comfy, so I slipped under my blue, fuzzy blankets, knowing that my room was where I was going to spend my last few minutes.

My eyes closed and my world went dark.

## FAILURE #3

I entered my room, closed the door behind me, and lifted my bed up enough to grab the tarp I had bought from the Dollar Tree earlier in the week. I took it out of its package and unfolded it, then laid it on the dark brown carpet.

I could hear the muffled screams of the birds outside my closed window as I thought, *Am I about to do this?*

I slowly walked over to my dresser and opened the second drawer, moved some of my clothing and grabbed the big bread knife I had hidden there.

Sitting on my bed holding the knife, I thought about the good times with the few friends I had.

*They will get over losing me.*

I laid down on the tarp in the middle of the white room and held the knife over my left arm. I moved the knife a little lower until I could feel the sharp blade touch my skin. After hovering there for a moment, I pushed hard and started to saw at my arm, inhaling sharply as the pain grew stronger and stronger. It stung like crazy, like I was getting a hundred shots all at once.

Sweat broke out over my chest and head. I lost my grip a little bit on the knife and readjusted it, then started sawing at my arm at a slightly lower angle. Blood started to run down both sides of my arm and pool there before flowing to my side.

*Enough for this arm.*

I stopped and laid there for a minute. My arm felt heavy and I could barely move it. It felt like I was trying to lift forty pounds when I grabbed the knife and brought it above my right arm, then lowered it.

I pushed down and started sawing back and forth again. At one point I pulled the knife up to see how deep it was. Blood started to trickle up and form around my cut, but it wasn't coming up fast enough.

*I have to go deeper.*

I put the knife back in the cut and started pushing it back and forth again while my right arm pulsed in unbearable pain and blood.

Finally, I stopped and put the knife to my side and watched the blood run down both of my arms. Then I just stared at the ceiling.

My room's light seemed to just fade away.

I started to fade away.


## FREEDOM

"I'm going to go biking with my friends," I tell my dad. He's doing work at his desk in the living room.

"You told your mother what you're doing, right?" he asks.

"Yeah," I answer.

I pull my bike out of the garage, and as I start to ride away, I think back on what happened throughout my school day, and how much I enjoyed it.

In English, we've been reading *Absolutely True Diary of a Part-Time Indian*. Hardly anyone in my class likes to read parts out loud, so today I volunteered to read four of them: the parts of the main character's troubled best friend, Rowdy, his nerdy friend, Gordy, his dad, and the girl he likes, Penelope. It's like an inside class joke when my teacher writes my name on the board for all of them.

It's so different from anything I've ever done before. For one thing, I used to never participate in class. I would sit back and watch people because I was too anxious to do anything social for fear that others would think less of me. And I've never enjoyed books before, but this one I can relate to. It shows that if you work hard enough, you can do whatever you want. And reading Rowdy's part is relevant to me because we both had it rough as kids and had to prove our worth.

Now I don't care what people think, mostly because this year I have friends at school. We hang out at lunch, we sit at a table together and talk about random things. I used to have to sit at crowded tables in huge lunch rooms. It was so loud I couldn't enjoy anything.

A lot has changed. After my first suicide attempt, my girlfriend's parents found out and took me to the hospital.

When my parents came they asked me if I had ever attempted suicide. I was honest with them, which led to therapy at least two times per week, sometimes three. I had to start trying meds, but the meds didn't work so I kept having to adjust them over the next couple months when the other attempts occurred.

But the biggest change happened when I came to Scriber.

Scriber is different because there are fewer students and everyone treats each other with respect. Teachers care about students in a different way. It's a more casual relationship. We call our teachers by their first names.

My math teacher, Mike, has a great sense of humor. My friends and I like to joke around with him and we have this "thing" about the "the Overlord." The Overlord is a gummy bear that rules over the room, and we put it in high places to watch over the class. We tell him, "the Overlord is watching over you," and he laughs uncomfortably at our creepy sense of humor.

I have fun with my classmates and teachers. That's worlds better than how my life was before. I feel comfortable. I like to be in conversations now and I barely feel anxious at all.

I'm feeling happy thinking about all of these things when I meet my two friends at the top of Main Street in Edmonds. We sit at the top of the hill on our bikes and contemplate how steep it is.

"We really shouldn't be doing this," one of them says.

"I'm doing it," I say, knowing that they know how stupid it will be to ride down the hill with the state of my tire, which had gotten bent on a sidewalk earlier.

"I'm gonna do it," the other friend says, who has a really nice bike.

My hesitant friend hands me his helmet, which will be my only protection if something happens.

I make the first move. I start peddling and say, "I'm going."

They follow, and before we know it we are all flying down the hill at almost 40 miles an hour, my shirt flapping like crazy, feeling freedom and adrenaline and happiness.

## A Note from Joey

I wrote this story because I had never told anyone about it or expressed what I went through. A writer from last year's Scriber book *This Is a Movement*, Nik Cook, came in and read his story about schizophrenic tendencies and suicide attempts to our ninth grade class. His story inspired me to write because I could relate. Talking about it was hard at first, but after I started it got easier and easier to unravel. Putting my story in a book is a step in a direction I've never been in before, and surprisingly it felt pretty good to write it down. I stayed after school every Tuesday and Thursday for a whole quarter to write this, and I don't even like to write. My decision to publish forced a conversation with my mother about everything that happened. I had been dreading that conversation for a long time because every time I thought about what I had done, I got really depressed. I thought talking about it would make me want to do it again. But I finally told her. She was surprised at the two attempts she didn't know about, and she thought it was a really good idea to write about it if it helped me get over the past. Coming to Scriber was one of the best decisions I have ever made because I am the happiest I've been in a long time. I know a lot of people will relate to my story—whether you are depressed and anxious or have tried some of the same things I have. I know that anxiety and depression kills any motivation for social interaction, but having friends and talking to people you trust in your life are actions that really do make a difference. Talking to people who listen and care about what you say makes living that much better. Bottling up your emotions works ... until it doesn't. My dreams for the future include traveling to many, many places. Ultimately, I want to end up in Australia.

## A Note from Joey's Mom, Mycca

Let me start by saying that I have not yet read Joey's story. It was important to him to wait until the story was published, and I wanted to respect that. Joey knows that this story is going to be painful for me to read, as it would be for any parent in a similar situation. I was surprised when Joey told me that he wanted to write about his battle with depression and suicidal thoughts. Normally, Joey hates to write, as well as talk about his feelings. I think he wanted to help others who were in similar situations by talking about his journey from a dark time into a positive and upbeat one. Joey also used writing this story as a means to help further his recovery into a healthier lifestyle. He is now far more active with friends, working out, and riding bikes, and he is attending school regularly. While Joey was writing his story, he talked with me about a suicide attempt that we were already aware of. When he told me that he had actually attempted suicide on three different occasions, I was shocked. I had no idea. How do you handle being told these things as a parent? Although it was difficult to hear, it was necessary to help begin the healing process. Our family has a number of individuals that have also struggled with depression, and in one case, actually committed suicide. Unfortunately, it has become normal for society to treat these topics as taboo, and for us to avoid discussing them. It is also common for people to downplay the amount of impact depression has on kids. Talking about the things contributing to depression, being supportive, and encouraging positive outlets are key steps towards returning to a healthy mental life. I hope that this story will encourage other teens who struggle to open up with a parent. Please do not let friends/family members that struggle with depression do so on their own. Don't wait until it's too late. Let's start a mental health revolution by talking about these issues. Don't give up, you are not alone.

# I ~~DON'T~~ LOVE YOU

## JENNALEISE JENSEN

*H*ow *do you know if what you feel is justified? How do you know your memories are real?*

These are the questions running through my head as I play with my seven-month-old niece, Ella, on the plushy floor puzzle. My younger sister is humming "Imagine" and strumming chords on the guitar to entertain Ella while three more of my siblings are in the kitchen making Thanksgiving dinner. We're waiting for our oldest sister to arrive with her boyfriend and our dad—my biological father—whom I haven't seen since before I was ten.

I'm sixteen now, and I'm scared. I'm scared because I don't know him. He's basically a stranger to me and I get the feeling he expects me to think of him as the greatest father in the world. Every time we've ever interacted since we moved away from him to Washington, he has not once apologized or owned up to anything he's ever done.

Ella looks up at me and her chubby cheeks spread wide in a grin. Her thin, short, strawberry-blonde hair is messy from a nap and she has green oval ring toys hanging over her ears. She's playing with her favorite light-up toy that has removable pieces and her little laugh rings loud with the sound of the running sink and pots moving in the kitchen. She's the one thing that can calm me down right now.

The only one that has seen my dad even somewhat recently is Annie— she's with him now. She took a road trip down to Utah and got to see him a few years before and kept in touch. When she heard he had to make a truck delivery for work in western Washington, she invited him to come for Thanksgiving with all of us kids—after my mom asked if we were okay with it. I said I was, but as the day came closer and I found out my mom wouldn't be there for the dinner, I wish I hadn't. It just seems backwards to me that I have to spend Thanksgiving with someone I haven't seen in years, rather than with my mom.

That was about a week ago.

I have very few memories of my dad. And even fewer that I believe, in retrospect, are actually good ones. What I know about him is from what my older siblings and my mom tell me. And up until a couple of years ago, I had always wanted to see him more often and thought the world of him. He could do no wrong. But I had heard stories that he would throw things at my older siblings and was verbally abusive, if not physically. It's enough to put me on edge. My parents were both raised in the Mormon church. But my mom left because she didn't feel comfortable raising six kids in the neverending suffocation of that religion and with the phantom of my dad's spirit looming over us, threatening us. So I'm reluctant to see him. Me being pansexual, demisexual, polyromantic, pangender and having a pixie cut with dyed purple hair—basically just emo and not open to him—is probably not what he expects. I know his opinion of me is going to change drastically.

When I see the truck come up the driveway, I feel my heart quicken. My stomach churns. My body tenses. I'm trapped in a web I never knew I fell into, and I am about to be consumed.

There's a knock on the door, and I do my best to snap out of it. My brother, Jerremy, sets a wet rag on the counter and comes out of the kitchen to open it. I glance up and take in the vaguely familiar 6'7" frame. My father's hair has gone from a grey salt and pepper to all white, and his strong build has become a bit gangly. He wears jeans and a slightly faded red T-shirt and a baseball cap.

In the spirit of Thanksgiving, we all gather around the living room and say "hi" to the new arrivals. Because of the number of people, some of us have to hug over the top of large couches hiding the red and yellow walls behind our group of ten. The greetings come easily and happily with Annie and her boyfriend, but when it comes to my dad, I freeze. He makes his way over to give me a side hug with his arm over my shoulder.

"Hey, Jen," he says. The churning in my stomach intensifies.

"Hi, dad," I reply. I avoid eye contact by looking at his chin.

"I missed you. I love you, Jenny," he says, feigning familiarity.

"I love and missed you too, dad."

It's a lie. I haven't missed him. I don't love him. My insides are being squeezed by the hand of some complex, sadistic emotion.

Guilt is trying to tear out my soul for saying those words. I've betrayed myself. I like to think I'm strong and self-assured, that I will stand up and speak my mind in any situation. But this is different. I've known of this man since I was born. He is the reason I exist. And that makes me sad. I wish he had never been a part of my life, or the life of anyone I care about.

The hug lasts much longer than I want it to, and as soon as it's over and I can leave without looking rude, I immediately go back to sit next to Ella on the floor. My sisters, Emma and Nia, sit on the couches in front of us, while everyone else migrates to the kitchen with *him*.

The feeling of helplessness is almost overpowering. Not being able to do anything about my situation makes my body constrict. I don't know how to handle it, so I just let it be. Small flashes cross my mind of when we lived in Utah and I was still a naive child: images of a dark apartment, Easter Egg Reese's Peanut Butter Cups, an elliptical, and the way he would stand with his back to the wall with his foot propped up against it. Of all that, I never remember him doing anything with us. I remember my mom and her boyfriend at the time taking us to a water park and letting us go to the playground across the street from our granny's house. But never anything with him.

What I do remember is a message he sent me after we got back from a week in Utah two years ago. It was the first time we had been back there since we left. *"Sorry Jenny that I can't see you while you are in Utah. I really wanted to, but your mom won't let me see you guys. I love you, and I hope that someday I will see you again. But I don't ever want to see your mom again!! Love you kids, Dad."*

At the time, I didn't understand it. He was the dad I idolized, but I felt like he wasn't putting in the effort to come see us. And I didn't understand why my mom wouldn't let us see him. Why didn't he ever want to see my mom again? How could anyone be mad at my mom?

Despite all the clues my family had given me, it wasn't clear just how bad my life could have been until one month ago during a family meeting.

My family was sitting in a circle when I came down. I was hoping I could stay upstairs for this, but they came for me anyway. It was somber in the garage. The Man Cave—where we watch comedies and football and listen to music. One comfortable couch, one rocker for when Ella came over, and twin Seahawks camp chairs. The designated "chill" area. The night before, my mom had fallen on her way to bed, and my brother thought it was because of drinking and told my sisters about it. That's why all of my siblings were gathered around the grey carpet—to hold a sort of intervention, to tell my mom we were worried about her. My sister Tisa and my mom sat in the camp chairs. Tisa was crying and holding Ella across her lap while Annie and my mom were involved in a heated discussion.

"You never tell us what's bothering you. None of you tell me anything," Annie said. Annie was rarely at the house because of two jobs and her boyfriend's three kids.

Emma was sitting on the floor in front of all of them. She was also in tears. Nia and I stood behind the couch where Annie and Jerremy sat. My heart felt like it was being squeezed into a spiked cage and my eyes burned.

"I shouldn't have to tell you what is happening with me," my mom said. Her eyes were watering and her face was blotchy, just as I'm sure my own was. "They're my problems and I won't tell you about them if I don't have to," my mom said while crossing her arms, leaning back and looking at the shelf to her right. She spoke as if she was defending herself from an attack.

"I am just concerned for you! I just want to make sure you're okay," Annie yelled. She was crying and desperate. "Does this have anything to do with dad?"

"Do not bring up your dad," my mom said, firmly. "Do not!"

"Why not? We need to talk about him. He's a part of this, too," Annie said. Her voice wavered slightly, but it was strong and powerful.

My mom scoffed and shook her head. "Fuck your Dad. He hasn't been a part of this for years! I am not talking about this right now," she said.

Nia slowly inched her way to the laundry room so that she wouldn't have to see what was going on. I didn't want to look either, but I needed to.

I felt hurt because I had never seen my mom so out of sorts when it came to my dad, and I felt guilty for holding an idealized image of him. For the first time I wondered if that had hurt my mom. The mom I love so fucking much, who never thinks she's good enough. She gives advice, accepts us for who we are, and has never pushed us beyond our limits. She took on multiple jobs to support six kids spanning an eleven-year age difference. She has always been our rock. She is the person I want to make the proudest, because she might finally realize that she is one hell of a mother.

Tisa looked between the two of them and said with a watery voice, "Guys, can we please not fight?"

"We are not fighting," Annie said.

"This isn't a fight," my mom said.

I walked into the laundry room and hugged Nia. We had never really shown a lot of affection towards each other, but we both needed it then.

My mom sat in her chair, her knee bouncing up and down, her face a stiff, emotionless mask.

"You guys know that he threatened to kill us, right?" Her voice shook. She still couldn't look at us. "Said he would take us up to a house in the mountains"—she paused and made quote marks in the air—"to 'protect us.'"

Silence reigned among the rest of us.

Mom's voice was wet and her chin was shaking. "He would have killed me to keep me from being with anyone else."

Nia started breaking down again, so while I just looked down at the ground, I rubbed her back.

Her words were like poison, eating away at my memories of him like they were a piece of paper in a fire. A dark and all-consuming flame that was beginning to engulf everything surrounding it, including any protection I had against my past and myself. I had known my dad was terrible to my mom, and occasionally, even my sisters and brother. I knew he called my mom names bad enough that I can't even say them, and said Tisa was a liar for something after our vacation in Utah. But I had never heard about his plan to kill us. I had been indifferent about him for the last couple of years after starting to realize that he wasn't the best dad and I avoided talking about him. But in that moment I felt fear. And anger. Everything inside of me sank to the bottom of the ocean, where it was dark and heavy and a hungry, desperate void.

All of my siblings except Nia nodded their heads and said they knew about it. Everything I was feeling before just amplified tenfold. I wished they had told me about something so important rather than letting me keep this image of a man who might have been my murderer.

*How much more is there that I don't know?* I wondered.

❦

Playing with Ella only works to keep me calm for so long. When my dad walks into the room and sits on the couch behind me, the panic and the fear creep up again. I start to breathe faster and I can feel my shoulders tense. Thanksgiving football is on, so he starts talking about the game with Beau. I do my best to tune him out until he mentions Ella.

"She's a cute little one, isn't she?" he asks. He's leaning forward with his elbows on his knees.

"Ya," I say back, nodding lightly. I don't want to talk to him. To be honest, I don't want him around her. It might be irrational, and I know Tisa hasn't said anything about it. She is his granddaughter, after all, but I hate thinking about what could have happened to us happening to her. It's been almost a month since I found out about who he really is inside, and I haven't been able to stop thinking about it.

Then he directs his words at me. "So how have you been, Jenny?" His voice is higher than I remember, and comes out in a slight rumbling tone that makes me shiver.

I want to yell at him. *I hate you! Just leave us alone and never come back! All we need is mom. I never want to be near you again.* Instead, I say, "Good. Nothing exciting."

The conversation goes nowhere after that. He starts talking to Emma, who is sitting next to him on couch and, like a few weeks ago, an empty feeling oozes into my chest.

❦

It was around one in the morning and the darkness of my room and the heaviness of my blankets was suffocating. I couldn't breathe. I was exploding and imploding at the same time. It was the Wednesday of mini-course week and we had finally started our identity monologues. Every semester at Scriber Lake High School, students can sign up for a weeklong class where small groups focus on one topic: acting, cooking, writing, college visitation, music, or specific periods in history. I chose to be in the social justice mini-course because all my life I've been angry about inequalities and I wanted to do something about it. The identity monologue assignment was a way for us to show others that we are more than just a race or sex. That we have stories and experiences and we are all alike in our differences.

Spending almost six hours a day discussing social justice issues and hearing about discrimination experienced in everyone's lives was emotional enough. But it wasn't just that for me. It was the reliving of the family intervention and the revelation about my dad that was keeping me up that night, taking hold of my throat and heart all week.

*I want it to stop already. Please just stop. Stop. If I die, maybe it will all stop and I won't hurt anymore.*

I knew I shouldn't be thinking this. Thoughts of suicide had always been passing—I had never honestly considered taking action before.

*I annoy my siblings.*

*My mom doesn't need to deal with all of us kids.*

*I would be helping her if I left.*

*I'm a burden.*

I thought of how I should go through with it—the best way to take my own life. The thought of my mom, my stepdad or any of my siblings finding me in the bathroom covered in my own blood scared me too much. I didn't want them to see me like that. No matter what. So my thoughts went to the medicine cabinet in the kitchen. Images of prescription bottles, ibuprofen and cold medicine were in my head for the next hour as I was trying to work up the courage to just get out of bed, walk downstairs, take a shitload of pills and lock myself in the bathroom to die.

*I'll sit by the tub on the white tiled floor and just look at random bottles and try to decide which ones to take first.*

But then I thought of my mom again, my number one protector and saving grace. The person who loved me the most, who gave the best hugs in the world. Even though the voices in my head were telling me that she would be better off without me, the overwhelming love I felt for my family—and the fear of breaking them—kept me from doing it.

My mom would be absolutely devastated at finding me gone; she would blame herself.

My family was the reason I stayed wrapped in my blankets that night.

I cried myself to sleep hating my entire being for even considering something that could have hurt my family so much.

Dinner arrives at the table. Turkey, gravy, salad, sweet potatoes. But I'm not excited about it. For the first time in almost ten years, I am eating at the same table as him and I hate it. I almost can't stomach anything. My eyes keep darting to him, then back to my plate.

The entire day, anxiety has been eating me up, but now it's at its peak; I can't make an excuse and leave without being rude to the rest of my family. I have to sit right across from him. Annie asks everyone if they want anything to drink and she even pours me and Nia a glass of champagne. It's bitter and leaves a terrible aftertaste, so I only have two sips. I've already had enough bitterness tonight.

A huge amount of food sits on my plate, and I almost can't finish it, but it's just too good. The sweet potatoes are my favorite—tangy, with cinnamon and orange zest.

"Make sure to chew a lot, you guys. It'll make more saliva and will help your digestive tract," Annie says. She's a dietician and always makes sure we know things like this. Everyone laughs, and I know her boyfriend will bring it up a few more times during dinner for more laughs. I love Annie.

I love everyone at this table. Except him. But I keep pretending. I keep forcing smiles because it's Thanksgiving and I don't want to ruin the day for everyone. It's Ella's first Thanksgiving and I don't want to tarnish it—even if she won't remember. So I go with it, even if I'm extremely reluctant.

It was Thursday, the second-to-last day of the mini-course, and we had finished our monologues that morning. It was time to read them out loud. We were going in a circle and when it came to my turn, I got the worst case of butterflies. There was cement churning inside my stomach and I felt a drop in my spine, like going on a downward swing with your eyes closed. I had shared my monologue with my teacher, Leighanne, that morning and told myself I would feel so much better after reading it out loud to the group. Even though I was excited, I knew it would be one of the hardest things I had ever done. No one in the class knew about the mental breakdown I was going through. Leighanne knew parts of it, like what happened with my family that weekend. But no one knew I had almost killed myself the night before.

When Tyler, who sat next to me, finished reading his story to us, it was silent for a minute to let the air rest. Everyone was crying and supporting the people in the room and, despite it being only our fourth day as a group, we all loved each other. I learned we all either had bad parents or shitty circumstances placed upon us. The feeling of community was unlike anything I had ever experienced. Now it was my turn to share. When people started looking at me in anticipation, I blew out a breath and felt the fluttering in my stomach hammer against my sides.

"Just a forewarning here. I'm going to be sobbing as I read this," I told them. And even then, I felt my eyes water as I looked down at the computer screen. It took a few seconds to start.

*"I don't think you understand—"*

I had to stop and breathe for another few seconds, but then Tyler and August, who were sitting on opposite sides of me, started rubbing my back and someone passed me a box of tissues. I put my face in my hands and then started again.

*"You have no knowledge of who any of us are, and yet you still keep asking. Asking to see us. Asking to keep us. You want us to be nothing more than beaten little things who would bow to your every whim. You wear a mask, a mask of Care Bear stuffed animals and warm hugs. I don't know if that was to keep us from seeing the truth or to keep you in our good graces for as long as possible. I don't even know if you honestly love us. But I have seen past your mask."*

I stopped for another second to breathe, but the back rubs and the support didn't stop. So I continued.

*"I am not who you want me to be. And I hope I never will be. You want me to be the slave of a monster, when all I am is a person. Not a good one. Not a bad one. I am just me. You threatened to murder us to protect us. You threatened to kill her to keep her. You wanted to take us to a house in the woods at the top of a mountain stocked up on shotguns. But I refuse to accept that. I will protect us."*

I was finally releasing all that had been building up for years. I felt like I was finally freeing myself from my demons. I told myself to keep going.

*"I do have a dad. But you are not him. And I am incapable of calling him*

*dad because of you. I wish I could, but I can't. You have forever ruined the title of dad for me. You betrayed that love.*"

My hands left my face and my voice sped up and got louder. I wanted to finish this. I needed to.

"*I will forever be your daughter, but will never again think of you as my dad. You are the prison of my mind and it's time for me to break free.*"

The weight I had been feeling on my shoulders since that weekend evaporated. My heart felt light and my tears kept flowing. I was right. I was better after reading it. I felt strong. And my letter was met with bowed heads and a sense of empathy throughout the room.

Everyone is finishing Tisa's chocolate pecan pie and raving about it while I sit in the living room watching *How the Grinch Stole Christmas* and think about how my biological father is stealing Thanksgiving.

I don't know if anyone else holds the same resentment as I do, I just know that I can't accept him. I will never trust him. Or love him. Or miss him. Since reading my letter out loud to my peers, I've felt like I gained power over the way he affects me. Like a veil of lies has been lifted and in its place is a sense of protection and control. I'm on my way to freedom.

*I can't wait for the night to be over. I just want to go home. I want the comfort of my bed. The solitude I get when I'm under my covers. I don't want to be around him ever again.*

"Come say goodbye, Jenny," Annie says. I stand up and walk over to the crowd in the dining area.

He comes over to me after hugging Emma and my stomach loses its sense of gravity.

"Bye, Jenny. It was so good seeing you again. I'll miss you," he says, lightly.

*I have to hug him again. I have to tell him I love him.*

I can feel the pain of guilt and the pull of the shackles on my heart as I put my arms around him and say the words I know I will never say again.

"Bye, dad. I love you."

### A Note from JennaLeise

Reading my monologue was the first step to seeing a way out of my dark place, and writing this story was the second. Now I'm in therapy and I'm getting stronger, even though there are days—even weeks—when I don't feel it. Writing this was also a way to tell my dad that I've given up on him and to get my mom to understand how much she means to all of us. It has been the hardest thing I've ever done. Knowing that my family will know I almost killed myself is my biggest fear. That night was the worst of my life and I know that having my family read it will bring up emotions I don't want to deal with, but without a doubt I know things will be better after. Writing is my way of expressing what I need to tell the world. I want people to read my story and come to an understanding that it is okay to speak out when you aren't comfortable with something. And I hope that after reading this, others will know that life can be shitty, but that there are always keyholes looking to the brightness outside of the room in which you are trapped. All you have to do is make a key. I plan to graduate a the end of next year and start an apprenticeship in general carpentry. Afte participating in building a tiny house with Sawhorse Revolution, I begar to visualize making a career out of that profession. The work was extremely satisfying because I could experience all of the aches and pains that go into making something for someone else; the thought of doing that for a caree seems like a very good path.

# RISING

## MONILINE WINSTON

*At first I was not willing to include the details of my trauma you're about to read, because I figured it would be too intense. Or maybe it was the fact that I was afraid to face the music, face my fears, in front of everyone. As I continued to type and edit my story to make it more true, more heartfelt, I realized I couldn't let my pain go if I didn't face it completely.*

*The goal written on my heart long before I had officially decided to start writing was to help others truly understand the pain of sexual abuse, even if only for a moment. Not for pity or sympathy, but for kindness and empathy. My purpose in life, however, is revealed within this story.*

*I want to reach out for all of the people like me, who have felt as hopeless and as useless as I did. This isn't a sad story, even with the tragedy in it. No, this is a story of strength, hope, and love. If you are in a safe, good place and are able to read this honest account of what happened, I invite you to do so. Stuff like this really does happen, and we don't have to hide it anymore.*

I look across the street at the group of kids dancing and chasing each other as we all wait for our buses to come—mine to take me to high school, theirs to take them to elementary school.

I want to be like them, my new neighbors: innocent, clueless, not a care in the world.

I would give anything to live one more day in which the only thought that darkened my mind was about the lack of basketballs at recess. When my only regret was over choosing the wrong thing for lunch, and when my whole world revolved around school and my backyard.

*That is how my parents wanted my life to be.*

As I look at my neighbors, laughing and twirling around, not afraid of being seen or judged, I know I can't be completely like that again. But that doesn't mean I can't be happy, or that I'm incapable of dancing like no one's watching. Or that I can't feel invincible again. In fact, with both my mind and my heart made of pure steel, nothing can truly get to me.

I'm stronger, and much wiser, than those kids.

The first signs of spring are all around me, including a warm sun smiling through the trees. With a deep breath of crisp air, I forgive myself, for the millionth time and for a million reasons.

*I forgive myself for waiting a year to tell my mother the truth. I forgive myself for trying to die. I forgive myself for the little girl I failed to save because I didn't step up first ...*

I look at the kids again, and this time wonder if they truly are innocent. Or maybe they're silently hurting, from something similar to what I've been through.

Maybe they will also have to travel their own road to recovery. Maybe they will have to stop trying to end their lives, to start talking about their pain, their own scars and how they got there. Maybe they will have to be removed from their homes, watch their parents go through rehab, watch their families be torn apart—all to heal from one moment of trauma.

It was the night of Valentine's Day—my favorite holiday, and though I was only twelve, even I knew it was a time of love.

I had worn my pink dress to school, given valentines to everyone in my sixth grade class, and had hidden a secret note in my crush's desk. A perfect day. I was so excited to see what my crush thought of my note that I couldn't sleep.

My mom, brothers, and I had been living in Ephrata for a few months, and I was finally feeling comfortable at my new school. My parents had officially separated, and life as I knew it was never ever going to be the same. As happy as I tried to be, nothing could fill the void; I was missing a big part of my life and identity when my dad wasn't around.

My mom's friends, Alley and Matthew, were living with us for a week or so until their house was ready in Everett. Alley and Matthew were staying in my room and their four kids and I were staying in my brothers' room—seven of us altogether. Alley and Matthew seemed like a couple that wasn't madly in love, but they were silly and strange in a way I admired.

I noticed right away that Matthew seemed fond of me. Throughout the week he told me how pretty I was at least once a day. One evening he walked in on me taking a shower, mumbled an apology that he thought I was his daughter, and left.

That night I was in the hallway, between the bathroom and their room. The door was open, and when Alley saw me, she gestured for me to come inside.

When I entered, Alley and Matthew smiled at me and asked if I wanted to watch *Family Guy*. At the age of twelve, that was my idea of "living dangerously" because my mom wouldn't let me watch it. They promised that it would stay between them and me, so I obliged, and almost instantly let my guard down. They seemed cool.

After they put on the show, they brought out a bluish-green pipe that looked like a tiny bowl. When Alley breathed out of it her breath was a milky white, which confused me. She put the pipe in my hands, and as I rolled it around my palm, she said, "This is like medicine you get at the store. It'll help you feel better. Here, I'll even hold it for you while you breathe it in."

She held it to my lips, where I reluctantly breathed in the sweetness of the pipe. When my breath came out foggy white, I couldn't help but be mesmerized because it looked so pretty against the light coming from the TV.

Alley giggled and said, "Don't worry, it does really work, and we don't have to tell your mom."

*Why not, then? There isn't harm in it as long as mom doesn't know*, I thought, and carelessly took a few more foggy breaths and watched the white smoke disperse through the air, along with almost all of my sense.

After Alley and Matthew realized I didn't get sixty percent of the jokes on *Family Guy*, but that I was laughing at them senselessly anyway, they began to ask me questions.

"Do you know what sex is?" Alley asked.

"I don't really know. My mom doesn't really talk about it," I answered.

"Do you have a crush?" she continued.

I bashfully told them about writing my crush the note for Valentine's Day and leaving it in his desk.

"Do you kiss him? Do you hold his hand?"

I was blushing. I was more interested in *Family Guy*, but their questions made me feel older and mature. The questions came all at once, too, so I could only keep up enough to answer the last one.

"Do you think you've ever had sex with him?"

I didn't really understand the question.

"Uh ... no, probably not. But we have hugged before."

After that, Alley and Matthew looked at each other, and then back at me. Then they left the topic alone.

Alley brought out some glow sticks, which I loved—especially the purple ones. As I twisted a few into a bracelet, she cracked hers open and a glowing green liquid gleamed against her skin in the dark. My eyes widened and she laughed and showed me how to do it to my own sticks. The purple liquid stuck on me like a tattoo and seemed bright enough to light my way through the whole house.

After the questions and the glow sticks, Alley left the room, saying she was going to the store and that she'd be right back.

When I was alone with Matthew, I leaned forward to continue watching *Family Guy*.

"How are you feeling so far?" he asked, casually.

It felt important that "Uncle Matt" cared enough to be concerned with how I was, considering I felt a little fuzzy, and sleepier than I was when I first walked in.

"I'm okay, I feel a little weird though," I said, suddenly concerned. "Am I supposed to be feeling this way? With that medicine?"

He scooted closer to me. "Yeah, you'll be fine. You feel better though, right?"

Forgetting for a moment how strange I felt, I smiled through it, and realized how giddy and carefree I really did feel. For a moment, I wasn't missing my dad, or bothered by when he left earlier that day, wondering how I was going to adjust, or whether or not my crush would like me back.

For just one moment, I was free.

"Yeah ... you're right, I do."

I continued staring at the screen when I felt the lightest touches against my side, and I whipped my head instantly over to him. He looked guarded, but not concerned.

"Are you okay? I can stop if you want."

I wasn't quite sure what exactly he was doing, but I assumed he just wanted a hug, and so I went with it.

"Uh, yeah, sure."

I let him stroke my sides. His fingers slowly trailed down to my legs, where he rubbed them. I was instantly uncomfortable, but maybe he was just trying to show me affection.

As he was rubbing me, his compliments of how beautiful my body was, how beautiful I was in general, and how my kids were going to be so beautiful made me more and more nervous.

"Do you really not know anything about sex?" he asked me, and I stared back at him. He was smiling slightly, and his eyes were a glowing blue.

I shook my head, not even knowing what to say, when his hand went up my stomach. "Well ... do you wanna learn a little? Do you want to know some stuff? We can stop whenever you want."

I shook my head as his hand cupped my chest, and gripped it, hard. I was so confused in that moment, because I wasn't quite sure why he picked there, of all places. I was in the middle of trying to figure that out when he slowly laid me down and began to pull down my shirt, revealing my chest. *Why does he want to touch me where my heart is?*

I looked down between my thighs and couldn't help but think, *Isn't he touching the wrong place? Maybe he really is just trying to hug me.*

So I let him touch my chest, and some parts felt sensitive suddenly, and I wasn't quite sure why. But somewhere between all that, and staring down at him while he was doing his thing, I looked around but I no longer felt like I was in the same place. My mind began to aimlessly wander into different sceneries, different stories, different people. It was like dreaming with my eyes open wide, against the light of the TV, reflecting off his eyes as well.

I had never seen eyes glow like that; they were brilliant bright blue that seemed to resemble the sky on a summer day. But when he looked at me so darkly, I knew in that moment that I would never be able to look at that color again.

My eyes begged not to open, but my duty to go to school beckoned. Once I did open my eyes and look around though, memories from the night before flooded into my head like waves of one big migraine.

My mind raced to make sense of it all, making my body stiffen, and my heart grow cold.

*Was it normal, what happened?*

*What exactly did happen?*

I got up, walked across the hall into the bathroom, looked in the mirror, and saw the fear in my eyes. It was strange how my own face suddenly scared me.

*Was that supposed to happen?*

I studied myself. The way my face appeared sunken, how I looked grim. The tears started to flow before I had even fallen out of my stupor. Only one small answer, a two-lettered word whispered through my mind and fell from my lips.

*No.*

*No.*

*No.*

*It wasn't.*

The confusion that had me feeling weak soon turned to horror—a realization that made me cry out, a sound I had never heard from anyone or anything in my life.

When I got to school I was emotionless; I did not care about anything, not even what my crush thought of my note. I sat stiffly in my chair and relaxed slightly to watch a science video, taking out my notebook and pen with shaking hands. I tore my eyes away from the video for a moment and realized I wasn't writing notes. Suddenly, the front and back of my notebook—and most of the untouched pages—were riddled with sharp scribbles:

*"Help me."*
*"Help me."*
*"Help me."*
*"Help me."*
*"Help me."*
*"Help me, please."*

Each plea felt like a blow, coming in waves and waves of devastation, but I didn't feel the pain. I felt nothing.

That afternoon I stepped off my school bus and hesitated before walking across the street to my apartment building. For a moment, I picked up my pace, thinking I was going to tell my mom what happened.

*Maybe she will understand. Maybe she can help me understand and make sense of it all.*

I was jogging slightly when I came to a complete stop. My home was right there, and my mom was so close. What stopped me was Matthew, who stood casually outside the front door, smoking a cigarette. When he locked eyes with mine his face was expressionless, indifferent to the fear written all over mine. I didn't even think, I just turned and ran. I didn't look back until I was at a safe distance. He continued standing there like nothing had happened. I stayed hidden until he finally sauntered into the house.

He and his family stayed for a few more days. During that time my confusion flared into a burning, fueled anger that shot through and circulated my body like blood. I was angry, and that anger quickly evolved into hate.

I hated Matthew, my mom, my dad, my brothers, my life.

But most of all, I hated myself.

I fell from a bright-colored, glitter-loving person into dark nothingness. For the next six months all I thought about was how blue his eyes looked in the lighting and the sound of his voice, and the only thing that seemed to relieve my stress was to run my hand up and down my arms, feeling my newly healing cuts. Something about the pain, hearing my blood dripping down onto the floor or the sink, soothed me. It made me feel human and alive.

Hatred for myself burned, but cutting seemed to somehow tame it momentarily. In the mirror, my eyes looked dead and black, but in those moments, nothing could hurt me. I didn't feel like a dirty girl who would let a thirty-year-old touch her in the first place.

I turned thirteen in the fall that same year, a year filled with cutting up and down my arms and riddled with suicidal thoughts. It went on for months until almost a year after Matthew hurt me. In early February, one night, I couldn't take it anymore and began to pour all my dad's prescription pills into one hand.

The note lying on the bed next to me simply read, *If you're reading this, I'm dead. If you hadn't taken advantage of me, I would not be dead.*

I wrapped myself in blankets smelling of strong, fresh linen and noticed that my white walls were tinted lavender by the moonlight and stars were seeping through my window. The chorus of crickets trickled through, too, and I smiled as I gently told myself, "The crickets are telling you to go to sleep."

My hands repeatedly balled into fists; I gripped my blanket like a vice, twirling it with my fingers gently, and thought about all the reasons I was done. From Matthew hurting me, to my parents' divorce, to my first heartbreak, to middle school in general, to feeling worthless and empty all the time, to cutting myself because I had no other release, I was done. Besides, in my mind, I would be quickly replaced by my new little brother, with whom my mom was pregnant. He wasn't my dad's, so I practically disowned him.

After I dragged my feet to the bathroom and swallowed the pills with a cup of water, I looked in the mirror, and the true horror of what I was about to do hit me like a train.

But my prideful smirk was still there.

*So, there.*

*Bet everyone's going to wish they didn't take me for granted.*

After a few minutes, my vision blurred. Soon every movement started to lag. Random objects, like my dresser, tilted gently back and forth.

*This is it.*

I began to shake and twitch.

*I probably should have tried to sing every song I've ever heard.*

My brain felt like it was spinning in my head.

*I'm going to be free in a second.*

My head, especially behind my eyeballs, burned and ached.

*If I'm an angel, I am going to sing every song I've ever heard.*

I burst into tears.

*I will never see my family again.*

*Who will protect my brothers?*

*My youngest brother won't even know me.*

I felt a pang of pain like a punch to the chest that made me wish, for a second, I could take it back.

Somewhere in between the sobbing and the silence, my shaky voice rang out, singing a *VeggieTales* song my Mom sang to me as a baby: "Think of me every day/hold tight to what I say/and I'll be close to you even from far away ..."

*My brothers are going to discover me tomorrow.*

The thought sent a new wave of panic and then pain to my body and an extra stab to my heart.

I cried until the only sounds were the voices in the night telling me to stay asleep.

*Mom, I'm sorry.*

❁

My legs pushed back and forth as I flew through the air on the swing. It was evening in Soap Lake, where the cliffs and desert look over the sticky lake that locals call "healing waters." The water near the shore glimmered a soft orange, mirroring directly from the sky, and the rust-colored cliffs that the sun rested on cast a black shadow over the lake.

*I shouldn't be here. I should've died that night six months ago. I should be dead.*

But I focused on my surroundings.

*My god, my home is beautiful.*

I smiled.

*No matter what anyone says, this is my home.*

I began to feel warm inside as I realized that if I had died, I wouldn't have had this moment to appreciate it. This place, my grandparents' house, which has always been "home" to me.

I had seen those cliffs, that water, throughout my childhood as I played there several times, but it seemed I was really seeing it for the first time. It wasn't just a distant drawing on a wall.

As the wind blew my thick hair onto my face, I realized that a part of me did die that night, and it died with any hope that I could be like everyone else around me. There was no turning back.

But this ... what was in front of me, wouldn't look as beautiful. Truly soaking it in, I let it warm my heart.

Hearing my brothers' laughing voices in the background, I was suddenly viewing this sight through tears because I knew they wouldn't be here either if I had died. If I had died, they wouldn't be celebrating, or happy, and more importantly, they wouldn't be cheering at me from behind to go higher. *Always aim higher,* I told myself.

*What if there are more scenes like this?* I ask myself. *What about France? Or Spain, or Britain? Surely there are thousands of things I have yet to see.*

My grin crept back onto my face.

*Besides, I still haven't sung every song I've ever heard.*

My little neighbors shove each other slightly while laughing, then turn their attention to the bus that has come to pick them up. Something about the kids' laughter as they board allows me to continue my forgiveness list.

*I forgive myself for every cut I ever gave myself, for every unkind word I've called myself to add fuel to my flames, for every time I silenced myself because I didn't want to find out what happened in the next chapter. I forgive myself for every time I didn't give myself the strength to see that I could get through all of this.*

With that, my breath is released, and I step onto my own bus. I slump into my seat and press my forehead against the cold glass window. When I see my reflection, I look at the features that have changed over the past two years.

I can *feel* it. I'm never going to be like those kids.

What was left from the wreckage, and what developed for the next year, was an opportunity for me to form who I truly was and what I really thought without anyone else's influence. A new acceptance of girls wearing shorts and crop tops, of social justice, and what relationships truly mean. A new value for life. A new view of beauty for the world, and the understanding that it wasn't my fault.

It was never my fault.

My heart changed for my parents, for myself. I felt something rising out of the ashes of my heart.

The old me, Abby Winston, was burned along with everything else I lost. I know I can't bring her back, but I can remember her as I grow older, and try to understand her better. As Moniline Winston, I will try to understand what more Abby could have done to save herself. And make sure that, on my watch, this never happens again.

I have to promise her that—it's the only thing that will ever put her to rest, that will get her to move on, finally.

As I continue to look into my reflection, I can accept that Abby is really dead, and that I am looking at Moniline.

And she is absolutely beautiful.

## A Note from Moniline

What I didn't understand at the age of twelve was that my mom was suffering from an addiction that she was struggling to break, and even when she went to rehab and had my baby brother, she went right back to it. I finally told a social worker the truth of what was happening, and I got taken away from her and sent to my father's. My mom was at her lowest point when she lost us. She was homeless, broken, and everything turned to dark. Until she started to get better, she went to rehab, she slowly came back to life. She found herself a home, and got herself into school, and regained custody of my baby brother. What warms my heart most—and ultimately let me forgive her and reunite with her—was that she did everything for her family. For me. For everything we've been through together.

Matthew is now in jail. What haunts me now is that in the year I didn't tell my mother what happened, he managed to hurt another girl when he moved out of the area. But because I reported it, my report solidified the case against him, which ensured that he would go to prison.

I no longer wish to be like everyone else around me, and I don't try to be. Even after everything that happened to me, I wouldn't change a thing.

Most people who don't know me well don't know what's happened to me, and they'd never guess otherwise. So, with that written in my heart, I love everyone, because I don't know their story or the demons they fight every day.

When people walk by me in the hallways, they don't know that I have thousands of words to speak and many, many stories I want to tell. These stories have changed my life for the better. When someone confesses to me that they had similar experiences, the first thing I tell them is what I learned through time. Life does get better. Things do heal, and one day, if you let yourself, you'll recover.

This story is for those that need help finding hope; my heart reaches out to you. This is for everyone out there who, like me, doesn't know exactly what happened in those traumatic moments, for those who feel like it was their fault. The ones that find relief in hurting themselves, the ones that feel trampled on over and over again.

My story is for understanding those it's too late to save, and for helping those that it's not.

*For my dad, Tyton Winston, August 1, 1974–September 27, 2018.*

## A Note from Moniline's Mom, Deb

In a time when my daughter was in crisis and needed me I was completely lost to my addiction. I did not protect her and I failed her as a mother. I am so proud of my daughter, who found the strength to live and then to stand up for herself and her brothers when she reported my drug use to protective services. Her testimony to police helped put her attacker behind bars. Her bravery to do all these things has set our family on the path that we are on now. It is the greatest privilege of my lifetime to be able to have a second chance to parent my children and make right the many wrongs. Active addiction is a horrific beast that destroys not only the addict but also their families and the children who are without a choice. As a family we suffered together because of my addiction; as a family we also heal together in recovery. It has been wonderful and an honor to be a part of Moniline's journey to work past her trauma. We cannot change the past, but we can work hard today for a better future tomorrow.

# THE WORST POSSIBLE NAME FOR A PERSON TO POSSIBLY HAVE

~~MADELEINE~~

~~MADDY~~

~~MATTIE~~

M

## ADRIEN ALLRED

Were backyards meant to be neat and tidy? Why were trees told to be straight as they can be, trimmed to fit in a lawn? Why was it when you thought of a yard, it was clean, and orderly?

Adrien wouldn't know, because their yard was the opposite of orderly, just like a lot of their life.

As they—or as society preferred, "she"—stood in the middle of their patio, looking out over the grass, partly green and mossy, with other spots yellow and dead because their sister had left her tent out for months on end, each thing that wasn't perfect reminded them of somethings and nothings all the same.

Sunshine should remind them of silence, but all their thoughts when the rays hit their body were dark thoughts, thoughts risen from the sewer system of their mind and through the passages of systems they thought they had known.

The sewer's water had been swirling and twisting for a long time, and though it was now settled more than it had been in a while, knowing that the conversation they were about to have wouldn't be a good one turned the water murky with dark thoughts. They knew they had to, though, but that didn't mean they wouldn't drag their feet a little, walking to the car where their mom waited from the backyard, instead of going quickly through the house.

*Keep yourself firm*, they told themself, *because if you don't the feeling will get worse.*

The feeling of discomfort that was always lurking beneath their skin.

Adrien's skin felt hot on their body, and their whole being would wash with the feeling. That was the worst feeling in the world, they were sure.

Adrien's days were built on comfortability, the little they could get. Pants loose enough to not stick to their skin, but tight enough to not hang. A loose shirt, no buttons or straps or multi-colored stripes. Plain. A flashlight in their bag, an extra pair of glasses just in case, as they never knew just how badly Mother and Father would react to anything. A backpack with straps that pulled equally on both shoulders, with their keys and a small first aid container neatly separated into another pocket. The little things. Things that wouldn't bother another person, but bothered Adrien.

They knew that as a fact: Adrien often got looks because they wore the same thing often until it was falling into unusable pieces, because it was familiar and easy and comfortable. Right now, it was a black hoodie their Father had given them, jeans, and a pair of Converse that were held together with duct tape and sheer luck, though that didn't help them on rainy days, when their socks would get soggy.

Adrien had been born a Madeleine, one of the worst possible names for a person to possibly have, in their point of view, which was very biased. But it was good in the sense that they could go as Maddy (which they thought of as Mattie often, since they were about twelve) without the bonus of telling their parents what gender they felt, or didn't feel, at that time. It wasn't perfect, but it was closer. Adrien always saw the dresses and skirts their mother picked and laid out for them, but pretended they didn't. Skirts were uncomfortable, always sliding unless too tight, and Adrien preferred fabric between their thighs so they didn't have to think about how their thighs felt when they slid together. Dresses were slightly better, in the sense that dresses stayed up, and could look pretty, but Adrien didn't like the fact that when they wore dresses, their mother would smile. Smile like she'd won. She hadn't won, not over them.

If Mother only smiled when Adrien did something she wanted, then Adrien wouldn't do it.

Adrien's mind was drawn to the tension of Sundays when they passed the dog's space, where they could see one of their sister's old-new flats poking out, the tip chewed off. Rae still hadn't learned to put her shoes away, and that was a constant reason for fights on that day between Mother and Father.

Sundays were the worst day, for Adrien.

Father would join Mother on Sunday, talking of his little "girl," and how amazing it would be if "she" took up going to church again. It had taken him a year of asking and Adrien replying "no" to get it, that this was one thing Adrien wouldn't bend on, but lately it had been picking up again.

"She" hated how the dress would make them look at "her" differently than if "she" wore shorts and a T-shirt. And even then, how people would look at "her" because "she" had long, tangled brown hair as opposed to short. The assumptions others made.

In the beginning, Mother would make Adrien come down to get in the car with their younger sisters, Lynn and Millie and Belle and Rae, still wearing their pajamas. Mother would take Adrien by the arm and make them walk into the church in their pajamas, everyone staring, feet stinging against the rough ground.

"Get changed, Maddy," she'd say, and handed them a dress.

Adrien had felt like crying, but they would move into the restroom, and put on the dress.

The next time it happened, Adrien was wearing Converse, unlaced and loose. The time after that, combat boots, and then Converse again. Adrien hadn't brought "appropriate" shoes, so they looked out of place anyway, among the dainty heels and flats or well-polished Oxfords.

Everyone seemed happier, but Adrien was sure that their discomfort was obvious.

Not that anyone noticed.

But maybe that was because that was how they spent most Sundays now, looking upset and uncomfortable.

Sunday afternoons used to be spent in the backyard, watching the second cousins chase each other around the trampoline. Adrien would lie on the ground, staring into the sun, thinking *Next time, I won't bend. Next Sunday, I won't.*

But they knew they would. Because Mother's word was law in this house.

Even more so than Father's, mostly because her words used to be rare and were now rising in count along with the firmness she put into them.

Adrien glanced back toward the house when they heard their Father's loud voice announcing that he was leaving now with the other kids, and startled slightly when they saw the small pile of plastic purple and blue lightsabers near the failed plantbeds, as Adrien had completely forgotten the sabers were there, with their head in the clouds, as it were.

Adrien knew that while Father's voice carried out of the doors, Mother probably wouldn't even call unless she saw Adrien face-to-face. That's the way it was, contact first, then get spoken to, often, unless it seemed there was an agenda, or she could see Adrien, or she felt she had to speak to them. Or, at least, that's how it seemed.

Father would jokingly call Mother the Emperor from Star Wars, when Adrien was a child, and then laugh and call himself "Darth Dad," or something equally father-like.

Or at least ... he had.

Lately any jokes were kind of taboo in their family's house.

The family's house had once been the Bardstones'. The room had once been Tyler's, if Adrien remembered correctly. Father would often remind them of things that happened with people like the Bardstones, the people before. Like Father's childhood friend and first love, who had committed suicide, and his friend when he was twelve who had used his dad's gun without permission and shot himself in the neck playing soldier. Father was the type to think that all the details were better than none, so all of the details were what Adrien got when they asked. He had stories for everything, truly, from why you shouldn't do drugs—"your great aunt and uncle went insane and committed suicide with the same gun because of pills"—to why he thought medicine and diagnoses were the most important thing—"my grandfather choked to death on his own vomit in an insane asylum because there wasn't good medication." Stuff like why he thought his church would take Adrien's *good and getting better* and make it *great and as fantastic as you can possibly be.*

Adrien was impacted by these stories in their own way—especially the ones that made Father cry—and they could understand them to the best of their ability. But his experiences weren't Adrien's, and not everything he understood could be transmitted into Adrien's life as the transmissions had been into his.

But at least Father was easier to talk to about some things. Yet, on the other side of the spectrum, there were the other things that he didn't understand, or didn't want to. Sexuality was a subject that was debated hotly, with Father's church-led beliefs that one should "give up" such "things," from homosexuality to Adrien's own asexuality, for Christ and the "life after," and Adrien's beliefs that those sorts of things were absolute bullshit. It was one of their most common things to fight about with Father. That and current events.

Adrien had been trying to come out to Mother for about four years, in different but similar ways to the one that they were planning to try again today, during the car ride. They'd never really even thought of gender as a thing until middle school, when the groups were obviously and sometimes forcefully separated from each other. It had taken Adrien months to really understand the differences society saw.

Other "girls" (their technical classification) in school began to wear makeup and fancy outfits.

Adrien didn't like that much.

The puffiness or tightness would make their skin itch, and itching was something they didn't want. Itching would lead to discomfort in their own skin, something they had already had enough of, thanks.

When they were twelve, they had grabbed their mid, navel-length brown hair and decided to cut it off. Mother wasn't happy with that. She'd agreed on them cutting it off some, but not that much.

Many years of "you're confused," and "not now" and "you are wrong" had left them with a soul-deep hatred for the words, and the things that the words were often attached to, even subconsciously.

*If this is so important to you, out of everything—then fuck that,* they wanted to say. But they didn't speak.

Years later, they tried to bring up cutting it off again, all the way.

But Mother didn't like that. "Your hair is so pretty, though," she had said, and though it wasn't worded in finality, it was a final decision.

When Mother spoke like that, Adrien had to listen.

Or, at least they had to pretend.

Mother wasn't there often, either. Even when she was there, she wasn't really. Hadn't been, in a while. She wasn't often there to force Adrien into the floral skirt and ruffled shirt.

Mother didn't know how to be comfortable. From cut pants with ironed shirts and clunky but tight shoes, Adrien really didn't know how

Mother managed to survive her job on a daily basis walking around in them. They'd seen the hospital where she worked; it was big and Mother tended to take the stairs instead of crowded elevators.

Or how she kept herself so immaculate and distant—physically and emotionally—in a proclaimed messy environment. She really wasn't a physical person, at all. And, it often seemed, emotions came the opposite of easily to her. Perhaps that mentality had saved her a lot when it came to being a doctor, but even at home she was often the same.

Her nails really were too perfect to ruin.

Yet, their house was run by those perfect hands, all of the two stories of blank-smelling home that it was. Either that, or it smelled of Father's perfume, which he put on like soap, excessively.

Adrien's nose twitched as they remembered that—they could actually smell the perfume lightly as they walked around the trampoline, past Mother and Father's bathroom window, which was open to the air. Father had probably put on too much again.

Father's personality was much like the perfume he preferred; he was loud and enthusiastic in both his likes and beliefs, and his dislikes and inner thoughts. He would speak on a normal day with both volume and happiness, but it was the days that he was quiet that Adrien came to think that something bad was going to happen, to him, or to them. Because, honestly, he was silent most of the time these days.

Adrien's mind pulled away from their previous thoughts. They sped up their walking a little to get closer to the gate to the front yard, backpack bouncing slightly against the back of their hoodie. They only allowed themselves to think again when they reached the end of the path, when they had to bend down to move the stones from in front of the gate, put there to stop their dogs from escaping through a hole in the side of the gate.

The front yard was cleaner than the backyard. But there were still things that stood out to Adrien as they closed the gate behind themself: a divot in the grass next to the gravel because Mother had pulled out the car weird on a muddy day, and Father's car, dusty, children's finger smears visible on the back windows.

Adrien's decisions had almost always been finalized in Father's car. Small conversations leading to such changes within themself, each time another part of them had just went, *Fuck that. Fuck him if he doesn't like it. What does that matter? Why does it matter if he thinks that one day, they won't be asexual? That one day, they will change, a switch will flip.*

That, Adrien guessed, was the entire reason for what they were planning to do today. They were going to tell Mother, and that was going to be that. At this point, all it was was common courtesy. They'd figured themself out, they were going to tell her because she was their parent. To Adrien, it was kind of simple. That would be the end of toeing the line, testing the waters, waiting for someone, something to change.

*If Mother didn't like it, fuck her*, they told themself. But they knew, if it came down to it, it wouldn't be so easy to turn and walk away. Honestly, they didn't know if they could do it. Cut the lines off completely. But they would, if it came to that. Adrien had known that for a long time now, and they were pretty sure their parents knew, too. It was pretty obvious, seeing as they kept a backpack pre-packed by their bedside. Just in case. That's why, when it came to those things, Adrien's parents had long since learned that Adrien's long-lasting "keep quiet" instinct would snap and they would get an earful of "fuck you's" and "fuck that's."

Adrien could feel something in their stride change as they walked forward, toward the car, where Mother, waiting, offered them a small smile. *Maybe she'd smile differently at them after.*

Their hands closed around the car handle and pulled, watching silently as it let out a click and opened, revealing Mother's light teal exercise backpack resting where they would sit. Adrien grasped it by its long, black straps and swung it into the back seat.

Adrien's heart began to rush a little harder, but this time, it didn't stop them from speaking—this time, instead of the pressure they swore they could feel in their throat stopping them, it pushed them forward.

They slid the chair a bit back before putting their legs into the too small car, feet crossed and stuck between the area where the door would close and Adrien's backpack, which they'd tossed in after opening the door. Before they had even sat down completely, just after they closed the door, their mouth had opened.

"You know, I don't really like the name I was born with."

Adrien didn't look at her as they said this, but what they needed to hear was in between Mother's words of greeting sputtering out and the feeling of eyes on their face as she backed out of the driveway.

Mother had pulled herself together somewhat by the time the car bounced slightly before pulling onto the road. She began talking about something or another, avoiding all that Adrien had just told her. But by then, Adrien had learned what they needed to know.

They could tell that Mother's eyes were a little colder on them, her body a little more stiff in its posture.

Shoulder against the window, watching the green trees move into and out of their sight, they sighed. Well, at least they'd tried. Adrien's mind moved on as they absentmindedly listened to the small talk their mother was attempting. But truly, Adrien had tried. And now, that was done.

It wasn't like it mattered in the long run, anyway. Adrien had given their parents the information required, if their parents had paid attention. *If Mother and Father didn't care to listen, then look for someone that does,* Adrien told themself. *Because you've always thought Mother and Father, in particular, wouldn't listen.*

## A Note from Adrien

I originally wrote this story as a fictional narrative for an assignment in Marjie's English class. I wanted to write a story for the Scriber book—I had heard past writers talk about how the process helped them, and I wanted that, too—but what is written here isn't even close to my original draft. When Marjie read this story, she asked me if it was true; when I read through it to answer her question, I realized it was. It wasn't fiction ... nearly everything had a tie to something I had tried and failed to write in my original draft for my nonfiction story. Some parts I had written were things I had known subconsciously and projected, and, after contemplating them, things I knew. Writing my thoughts and experiences was easier than trying to find a way to communicate them verbally; writing fiction has always been an escape for me. Writing this story as fiction helped me understand myself so that I could then tell my parents who I really am. I was able to talk to both of my parents when the story was done. The words were already there so I could actually communicate the basics in a way that was understandable to them, even if they couldn't understand it completely. This experience reinforces my desire for my stories to get out there. I want to write stories that bring understanding to people living in the margins, turn them into screenplays, then, hopefully, help with the film.

# FREEBIRD

## ARIEL SANABRIA

My sister, grandma, cousin, and I walk into the church feeling self-conscious, like we are disrespecting the ceremony by walking in late. More than two hundred people seem to be staring at us. What makes it worse are the high heels my sister is wearing—every step sounds like a stomp. In that quiet moment the last thing I want is more attention, but Chris Brown, my teacher and close friend, smiles at us and makes us feel safe.

"What we are doing is pouring water into this bowl," he says, addressing us, "and while you pour the water you can say one word that describes Liza." He stands in front of the church, over six feet tall and wearing a flowered shirt and khaki pants, holding one hand behind his back. He smiles at us like he is happy to see us.

Without hesitation, my sister walks to the front of the church—the size of a basketball court—and pours a glass of water in the bowl. The skylights are letting daylight in and the evergreen trees tower over, as if they, too, are in the memorial service. In the background the sound of Japanese ukulele music plays.

"Wisdom," my sister says, then returns to her seat as people continue to make their way to the front.

Still in the first stage of grief, I can't help but deny the fact that Liza is really gone. I feel hesitant to go up and describe Liza in one word, but if I did, I would definitely say "Warrior." She had the ability to show others something inside of themselves that they never knew existed. She taught me about myself. She taught me I was an artist, that I loved nature, and how to cope with stress.

Liza's sister walks to the front to sing. I can see that Chris is in a lot of pain, but Chris is still Chris—with a big smile, shoulders hunched over and hands behind his back, he takes his seat in the front row. Chris was a guardian to Liza. They ran an outdoor education program together at Scriber called InStep, a class in which fourteen students spend a whole quarter in nature. My sister was in Liza's last InStep group before she got really sick from multiple myeloma, and I was in it last year without her. Liza begged me to sign up when I was in her art class, but I kept saying "no" because hiking wasn't something I did. Somehow I ended up on the list, though, and I have a feeling Liza was behind that.

Now, I can't imagine my life without experiencing the silence that gives me the feeling of freedom. Nothing but the sound of my heart pulsing, breathing as if the air is limited and at the same time pure. Every day I walk outside smelling nothing but exhaust fumes or burning oil. Not out in nature, though. Even the wet and cold doesn't bother me—it's like a sense of empowerment that gets me moving and I have no feeling of pain. The life around me gives me energy, a pulse of adrenaline coursing through my veins, keeping me warm.

Liza gave me that gift; she knew me better than I knew myself. She knew what I needed.

A mixture of friends, family and students take turns going to the front to tell stories about Liza. Chris tells a story about waking up during an InStep trip to Orcas Island to see Liza doing yoga by the water at sunrise. My English teacher says she knows Liza is here, listening in a way "not humanly possible," like she was known for doing her whole life. Santino, a former student, talks about how Liza would always compliment his artwork and tell him that he had talent. I can relate to all of these stories in some way.

But then Antonio, a part of my InStep group, makes his way to the front and I'm surprised. I don't know what he's going to say because I know that he had issues with Liza. He tells everyone that he wasn't planning to speak, but as he sat there listening to everyone else, he knew he had to. "When I first met her, we weren't close. We didn't really get along," he explains. But then he mentions a card Liza wrote to him for graduation. "You're going to go to college and be successful," it said. He says he cried when he read it because he expected his mom to be there and say that, and instead it had been Liza. She even remembered that he wanted to be a computer programmer. "You may not like me, but I still like you and I wish you the best," she had written.

*That's so Liza*, I thought. She saw the good in him, in everyone, and in every situation. She never let things get to her. Like Antonio, I held back with Liza at first, too. When I was in her class freshman year, I would not do any of the class assignments. Instead I did my own thing, kept my head down, and hoped that she would forget and ignore me. But she kept pushing to the point I got annoyed. At the time I didn't know what was wrong. Was I stressed? Depressed? Or was I just angry? What I was feeling didn't matter. I just wanted to feel better. Liza knew what I needed. She had a secret ability to feel someone's energy. She wrote me a pass to walk around the whole school, on a trail surrounded by nature—a trail she showed our class at the beginning of the quarter, dominated by evergreens and Western red cedars. The first time I went, I thought it wasn't going to change the way I was feeling, but halfway into it I forgot the reason why I was walking in the first place.

Now I only think about living out of a big backpack. Everything is so simple when all you need to live is broken down to a basic formula that anybody can read. No Facebook or Instagram, no artificial sounds or pollution. I used to feel trapped in the modern city, like my arms and legs were tied and that I was expected to do what everybody else was doing: go to school, get an education, work, and then die. Hell no. Because of Liza I know I can walk in wide open places feeling free as a bird.

Who would've thought that a couple of hikes could alter someone's life? I went from being depressed every day to being close to alright. If it wasn't for Liza begging me to join, I would have remained that person hiding in the corner.

As the sharing part of the service ends, I'm drawn to a painting in front of the church. It contains waves filled with blue, orange, red and yellow, representing the beauty of water. It reminds me of the time I heard the ocean during an InStep hike in the Olympics. I heard an amplified sound of the aggressive waves when they hit the ground in a loud splash then rebounded, taking every sand and salt grain back to the ocean. I listened as the ground slowly transformed, from mud and dirt to sand and gravel. And then, finally, I saw it: the ocean, and a horizon that reached no limits. I saw the actual curvature of our earth and felt awe looking at the contrast of dark shadows and bright grey sky. As the ocean tide slowly increased we moved our way to the south, keeping the ocean on our right, sinking into the fine sand in a slow, crucial workout.

A slideshow of pictures from Liza's life flashes on the eight monitors surrounding us. In every picture she is doing something—hiking, biking, traveling, swimming, smiling—and she's always surrounded by the people she loved. I realize the service is almost over, and I'm going to have to face the reality of one of my biggest inspirations being gone.

In one of the pictures, Liza is hiking through a wooded trail, and I remember the narrow fresh-cut wood plank trail during one of our InStep hikes. The trail is shadowed by dark trees that tower overhead. On that trip I learned that when trees die, they don't just disappear; they slowly decompose and eventually feed other plants, helping them grow. They become nurse logs, continuing the cycle. As the service comes to a close, I'm realizing that Liza is my nurse log. She taught me and helped me grow, and even though she's gone, she will continue to feed me and be with me.

The pastor of the church goes to the front and says some closing remarks. Jazz music plays and everyone begins to make their way to the back for the reception. I think about a story Chris told us during our backpacking trip. It was pouring down rain and everyone was soaking wet. Chris said, "We don't have to do this. There's always something in class that we could do." It was like he was asking for our permission about whether or not we would go. Our group was confused. "Are you kidding? Of course we are doing the hike," one person said. Chris, with a smile, told us a story about the University of Washington rowing team and how they decided that, however bad the circumstances became, they were going to "embrace the suck." No matter how terrible things got, they knew that making it through would only make them stronger. Our group, without a second thought, put our hands in the middle, raised them up and screamed "EMBRACE THE SUCK!" then proceeded to our hike in the pouring rain. We said that phrase for the remainder of the trip and even had "Embrace the Suck" T-shirts made. From that moment on I have always reminded myself that when times get difficult, "embracing the suck" will only make me stronger and better overall.

At this moment I know that Liza wouldn't want me to feel sad or sorry. If she were here, she would definitely write me a note to take another walk. She would want me to embrace the suck.

## A Note from Ariel

Mine is just one of the lives Liza has affected and touched. Because of Liza's urgency for me to join InStep as a junior, I was able to repeat it this year as a teaching assistant. I am a graduating senior, and just found out I was awarded a Washington State Opportunity Scholarship that will cover my education for the next five years. I will begin by earning an Automotive Service Excellence (ASE) certificate at Shoreline Community College, and decide what to do from there. When Chris Brown heard the news, his response was, "Do you know who is smiling?" I plan to continue hiking every chance I get because I know that it will always make me feel better when times are low. Liza's legacy really shows what one person can do; I will remember her and what she and the outdoors have taught me for the rest of my life.

*Excuse me while I kiss the sky.*
—Jimi Hendrix

# ABOUT SCRIBER LAKE HIGH SCHOOL

Scriber Lake High is a public school of approximately 200 students in the Edmonds School District, located just north of Seattle. We are one of Washington's oldest alternative schools. Scriber is a school of choice; some students come to us as freshmen, and some come seeking a second, third or fourth chance to graduate. A majority of our students have struggled with depression, anxiety, abuse, loss, homelessness, or drugs and alcohol, and have been lost in the educational system because of these outside factors.

In 2012, our staff accepted a three-year challenge to increase our students' sense of self-efficacy and resiliency through the use of Appreciative Inquiry questioning techniques. Under the leadership of Dr. Cal Crow, Director of the Center for Efficacy and Resiliency, we challenged ourselves to create a school filled with heart and soul—a school focused on supporting students' stories and dreams for the future.

In 2015, we published a book about our journey called *Creating a Success Culture: Transforming Our Schools One Question at a Time.* In this book, we tell anecdotal stories of how we changed conversations with our students to bring them back into the center of their own education. Our book is available on Amazon, and we invite conversations with other schools working to address the needs of students impacted by childhood trauma.

# FURTHER READING: BIBLIOTHERAPY AND THE SCRIBER BOOKS

## LEIGHANNE LAW

"I loved the Scriber books—what should I read next?"

For the past five years, I've been asked this question at least once a day. When it comes down to it, the Scriber books are the most hardworking series I've come across in my nearly fifteen years as a bookseller and teacher-librarian. Time and time again these slim volumes have proven themselves to be gateway books that transform reluctant readers into voracious readers.

How? These stories speak directly to students' lived experiences, giving voice and validation to what they once presumed should be silenced and shamed. With authenticity and radical acceptance, the stories in *Listen* explore mental health, gender identity and expression, family dynamics, issues around immigration, sexual abuse, grieving, and addiction. They are always my first prescription for bibliotherapy—the practice of using books to heal.

But what do you recommend to someone who has read every Scriber book and is clamoring for more? How do you keep the fire fueled? My solution: a go-to list of further reading like the Scriber books, organized by theme:

Processing Death or Loss
- *They Both Die at the End*, Adam Silvera
- *We Are Okay*, Nina LaCour
- *The Hate U Give*, Angie Thomas
- *The Beauty that Remains*, Ashley Woodfolk
- *Essential Maps for the Lost*, Deb Caletti

- *The Boy in the Black Suit*, Jason Reynolds
- *Long Way Down*, Jason Reynolds
- *Bearing the Unbearable*, Joanne Cacciatore
- *Kids of Appetite*, David Arnold
- *Some Kind of Courage*, Dan Gemeinhart
- *Life in a Fishbowl*, Len Vlahos

Addiction
- *Tweak*, Nic Sheff
- *We All Fall Down*, Nic Sheff
- *The Crank Trilogy (Crank, Glass,* and *Fallout)*, Ellen Hopkins
- *Forged by Fire*, Sharon M. Draper
- *Beneath a Meth Moon*, Jacqueline Woodson
- *Gabi, a Girl in Pieces*, Isabel Quintero
- *Rodent*, Lisa J. Lawrence
- *Finding Hope*, Colleen Nelson
- *This Is the Part Where You Laugh*, Peter Brown Hoffmeister
- *The Way Back*, Carrie Mac

Sexual Abuse and Assault
- *A + E 4Ever*, Ilike Merey
- *The Gospel of Winter*, Brendan Kiely
- *Exit, Pursued by a Bear*, E. K. Johnston
- *Speak*, Laurie Halse Anderson
- *Hunger*, Roxane Gay
- *The Female of the Species*, Mindy McGinnis
- *Asking for It*, Louise O'Neill
- *Jaya and Rasa*, Sonia Patel
- *Take It as a Compliment*, Maria Stoian

- *I Have the Right To*, Chessy Prout

Gender Expression and Identity
- *Every Day*, David Levithan
- *When the Moon Was Ours*, Anna-Marie McLemore
- *Symptoms of Being Human*, Jeff Garvin
- *The Body Is Not an Apology*, Sonya Renee Taylor
- *And She Was*, Jessica Verdi
- *Freakboy*, Kristin Elizabeth Clark
- *Gender Outlaw*, Kate Bornstein
- *Parrotfish*, Ellen Wittlinger
- *Love Beyond Body, Space, and Time*, Hope Nicholson
- *Beyond Magenta*, Susan Kuklin
- *The Gender Quest Workbook*, Rylan Jay Testa et al.
- *The Prince and the Dressmaker*, Jen Wang
- *The 57 Bus*, Dashka Slater

Family Dynamics
- *Between the World and Me*, Ta-Nehisi Coates
- *Fun Home*, Alison Bechdel
- *Are You My Mother?*, Alison Bechdel
- *Hey, Kiddo*, Jarrett J. Krosoczka
- *Everything I Never Told You*, Celeste Ng
- *When Dimple Met Rishi*, Sandhya Menon
- *Losers Bracket*, Chris Crutcher
- *I Am Not Your Perfect Mexican Daughter*, Erica L. Sánchez
- *Blood Family*, Anne Fine
- *Fire Color One*, Jenny Valentine
- *The Memory Trees*, Kali Wallace

- *Same Family, Different Colors*, Lori L. Tharps
- *The Education of Margot Sanchez*, Lilliam Rivera

Immigration
- *In the Country We Love*, Diane Guerrero
- *The Distance Between Us*, Reyna Grande
- *Americanized*, Sara Saedi
- *An Indigenous Peoples' History of the United States*, Roxanne Dunbar-Ortiz
- *This Land Is Our Land*, Linda Barrett Osborne
- *American Street*, Ibi Zoboi
- *Enrique's Journey*, Sonia Nazario
- *Saint Death*, Marcus Sedgwick
- *Tell Me How It Ends*, Valeria Luiselli
- *The Line Becomes a River*, Francisco Cantú
- *Born a Crime*, Trevor Noah
- *A Girl Like That*, Tanaz Bhathena

Mental Health
- *The Body Keeps the Score*, Bessel van der Kolk
- *The Art of Feeling*, Laura Tims
- *Suicide Notes*, Michael Thomas Ford
- *Challenger Deep*, Neal Shusterman
- *The Memory of Light*, Francisco X. Stork
- *Eating Mindfully*, Susan Albers
- *Madness*, Zac Brewer
- *Turtles All the Way Down*, John Green
- *Highly Illogical Behavior*, John Corey Whaley
- *The Rest of Us Just Live Here*, Patrick Ness

- *Six of Crows*, Leigh Bardugo
- *Fans of the Impossible Life*, Kate Scelsa

# ACKNOWLEDGMENTS

We have so many people to thank this year. Tim Holsopple spent hours of volunteer time poring over this book in order to meticulously, yet gently, edit it. Taylor Erickson, our counseling intern, legitimized our program with research, numbers and an amazing term paper, and is responsible for collecting the Scriber writers' quotes from 2012 to the present. Local recording artist Scarlet Parke shared her music and time, Karen Mikolasy brought groups of University of Washington teacher candidates to listen to our kids' stories, and José Gonzalez's work with ancient Aztec ideas inspired our theme and writing process.

As for the Edmonds community, we recognize how lucky we are to have this "village" supporting us. The Edmonds Kiwanis and the Rotary Clubs of Lynnwood, Alderwood Terrace and Edmonds are consistently wonderful to our school. Bob and Mele Fuller continue to be superb community fans, and Haifa Alhussieni of Cafe Louvre has graciously hosted our book readings every year since 2013. Dr. Cal Crow continues to be our "Question Master" in all things, and we appreciate his availability. The Edmonds School District maintains its support in all ways, with special thanks to Superintendent Kris McDuffy and Scriber Lake Principal Andrea Hillman. Many thanks to Andrea and to Chris Kratz for their editing clean-up work and to Sky Gates for the title inspiration.

Our greatest thanks, however, go to the Scriber writers' parents, who show so much courage in supporting their children.

We are grateful.

# ABOUT THE EDITORS

**Marjie Bowker** has taught at Scriber Lake High School for twelve years out of her twenty-one-year teaching career. She landed at Scriber after teaching in local "general" education positions and at American International Schools in Norway, China, and Vietnam for nine years. She did not intend to stay at Scriber long; however, she quickly fell for the honesty of the students and soon realized she had found her place. This is the seventh book she has compiled and edited with Scriber writers. Marjie is the author of a curriculum guide, *They Absolutely Want to Write: Teaching the Heart and Soul of Narrative Writing*, and a book based on the concepts of Appreciative Inquiry, *Creating a Success Culture: Transforming Our Schools One Question at a Time.*

**Leighanne Law**, Scriber Lake High School's teacher-librarian, earned her BA in English from Carleton College in Minnesota and has used her degree to build a career out of reading and talking about books. After many years working as a bookseller and event coordinator, she realized that the best part of her job was connecting youth to the glorious world of reading. In 2013, she went back to school to earn her MA in Teaching from the University of Washington and then jumped right into their library endorsement program. One of her professors at the UW told her about this amazing little "alternative" high school that was looking for a new librarian and in 2014 she landed the best job in the world. She is honored to be a part of this school's community of storytellers.

*Compassion is the radicalism of our time.*
—Tenzin Gyatso, the 14th Dalai Lama